One Room

SCHOOLS AND SCHOOLTEACHERS
IN THE PIONEER WEST

GAIL L. JENNER

TWODOT®

GUILFORD, CONNECTICUT
HELENA, MONTANA

A · TWODOT® · BOOK

An imprint of The Rowman & Littlefield Publishing Group, Inc.
4501 Forbes Blvd., Ste. 200
Lanham, MD 20706
www.rowman.com
A registered trademark of The Rowman & Littlefield Publishing Group, Inc.

Distributed by NATIONAL BOOK NETWORK

British Library Cataloguing in Publication Information available

Library of Congress Cataloging-in-Publication Data
Names: Fiorini-Jenner, Gail L., author.
Title: One room : schools and schoolteachers in the pioneer West / Gail L.
  Jenner.
Description: Helena, Montana : TwoDot, [2018] | Includes bibliographical
  references and index. |
Identifiers: LCCN 2018018494 (print) | LCCN 2018028111 (ebook) | ISBN
  9781493036691 | ISBN 9781493036684 (pbk.) | ISBN 9781493036691 (e-book)
Subjects: LCSH: Rural schools—West (U.S.)—History. | Education, Rural—West
  (U.S.)—History. | Pioneer children—Education—West (U.S.)—History.
Classification: LCC LC5147.W47 (ebook) | LCC LC5147.W47 F56 2018 (print) |
  DDC 371.009173/4078—dc23
LC record available at https://lccn.loc.gov/2018018494

♾™ The paper used in this publication meets the minimum requirements of American National Standard for Information Sciences—Permanence of Paper for Printed Library Materials, ANSI/NISO Z39.48-1992.

Printed in the United States of America

This book is dedicated to those vigorous schoolteachers who taught in one-room schools and who might have only been slightly older than their students, and also to those small, one-room (and, in some cases, two-room) schools that became the center of their community's public life. Most of these structures have been abandoned or destroyed, but some still exist—as museums, community centers, as homes—and even as ever-evolving schools within their more modern communities.

Contents

Acknowledgments vi
Introduction: The One-Room School 1
The Three "Rs" in One-Room 8
Schoolteacher Stories 19
Moving West 32
    Alaska 34
    Arizona 40
    California 44
    Colorado 69
    Idaho 74
    Kansas 78
    Montana 84
    Nebraska 92
    Nevada 100
    New Mexico 104
    North Dakota 108
    Oklahoma 115
    Oregon 119
    South Dakota 131
    Texas 135
    Utah 143
    Washington 149
    Wyoming 154
Epilogue 158
Bibliography 161
Index 165
About the Author 181

Acknowledgments

First, I would like to thank my editor, Erin Turner, who worked with me tirelessly on this project. Her help in this and past endeavors has been above and beyond wonderful! And thank you to everyone at TwoDot books.

Secondly, I want to thank all those who assisted me. After sending out invitations and requests for stories and anecdotes regarding one-room schools and those who attended them or taught in them, I was thrilled at the number of individuals who responded. The heartfelt responses and stories were a great tribute to the history of schools and education over the last one hundred years and more. Thank you to all those who sent me contributions, whether through personal interviews, online responses, or written history. The following represent those who took time to send me information in addition to family or local stories. If I have omitted anyone, please know that there were dozens of people's stories that might not have made it into this volume because of space or other requirements, but I am sincerely grateful for every contribution.

Ann Allen
Stephanie West Allen
Sam Alvord
Deborah Anderson
Arcanum Wayne Trail Historical
    Society, Inc.
Rose Atondo
Patti Barker
Sharon Barni
Tessa Benkosky
Grace Bennett
Lori Bennett

Gay Berrian
Diane Biggar-Taylor
Kristi Schluter Bigham
Bruce and Vonita Bishop
Mary Blake
Debbie Hardin Bowling
Teresa Branch
Natalie Bright
Brenda Brodmerkle
Irene Bennett Brown
Victoria Bunce
Rochelle Burroughs

ACKNOWLEDGMENTS

Judy Bushy

Betty Davis Carrier

Jeri Christopher

Genetta Clark

Donald Collins

Jim Cook

Naomi Liz Cooksey

Sherry Coonrod

Lilliane Conner

Wayne Courts

Lee Craig

Bev Caban Cross

Clint and Pat Custer

Terri and Mark Davis

Elaine Davis

Tammy and Andy Dean

Michelle DeLaney

Peg Delugo

Virginia N. Dove

Andrea Downing

Laura Drewes

Peggy Margaret Ellenbecker-Nietfeld

Jennifer Embury

Lora Facey

Sharon and Steve Farrington

Nancy Fine

Fiddletown Preservation Society

Karen Casey Fitzjerrell

Fort Jones Museum/Cecelia Reuter

Melanie Fowle

Hazel Gendron

Sandy Gibson

Lisa Gioia-Acres

Mark Greenfield

Carolyn Wing Greenlee

Beverly and Barbara Gust

Betty Hall

Monica Jae Hall

Carol Harper

Punky Hayden

Ruth Hensell

Stefanie Hunt-Linsley

Demetrios Iannios

Kaitlin Ikenberry

Kristina Jackson

Loretta Y. Jackson

GloryAnn Jenner

Jack Jenner

Corri Jimenez

Sheridan Johnson

Trinity Jones

Brenda Kelsey

Frank Kelso

Jane Kirkpatrick

Kathy Koon

Danielle Koresh

Linda Ladd

Page Lambert

Lynn Milburn Lansford

Patricia M. Laustalot

Virginia (Ginny) Laustalot

Jean Lesmeister

Alicia Lewis

Fran Lewis

Priscilla A. Maine

Norm Malmberg

Carol Maplesden

Larry Maplesden

Lana Marie

Marlene and Charles Martin

ACKNOWLEDGMENTS

Roy Martin
Cynthia Leal Massey
Betty Trueax McClelland
Betty McCreary
Roni McFadden
Lisa Stricker McFarland
Janet Meranda
Doris Miller
Rebecca Hawkins Mills
Doreen Mitchell
Lisa Moberg
Kathy Moore
Cicely Muelrath
Vella Munn
Carol Murphy
Native Daughters of the Golden West,
    Eschscholtzia Parlor No. 112
Julie Newberry
Shirley Newberry
Lois Kennedy Newcomb
Karen Nicholson
Katherine O'Connor
Lorraine O'Connor
Lillian Ostendorf
Karen Paige/library.ca.gov, California
    History Room of the California State
    Library, Sacramento
Lola Pearce
Linda Persson
Patricia M. Peterson
Angie Pettit
Lanora Phelps
Patty Philps
Mollie Phipps
Padi Pierce

Patsy Piersall
Harriett Quigley
Chuck Rabas
Leslie Ralston
Jason Rasmussen
Stephanie Tickner Reynolds
Margaret Ritches
Shirley Ross
Irene (Cindy) Sandall
Sandy Sandall
Shari Fiock Sandahl
Peggy Sanders
Carolyn Sato
Linda Scallon
Betty Lou Schott
Hank and Beth Schott
Madelyn and Gary Schott
Anne Schroeder
Bev Scott
Debbie Baker Scott
Sarah Secrest
Amy Woods Seelbach
Marilyn Seward
Dawn Shlaudeman
Michael Shreeve, Sr.
Cathie Herman Schoer
Kayann Short
Kathryn Shorrock
Vicki Simmons
Perry Sims
Siskiyou County Museum
Steve Sloan
Roy Smith
John Sorensen
Annette Stewart

ACKNOWLEDGMENTS

Alan Stevens

Jean Thorson

Heidi M. Thomas

Bernita L. Tickner Collection

Laurie Ann Tippit

Barbara-Leigh Tonelli

Jose Torres

Alice Trego

Susanne Twight-Alexander

Marsha Ward

Shawn Watt

Beverly Wenger

Christine West

Dennis Weston

Joe and Jennifer Wheeling

Robin Wiedl

J. T. Wilcox

Louise Wilson

Dan Worley

Jolyn Young

Elaine Zorbas

Bob Zybach

Introduction: The One-Room School

IT IS HARD FOR STUDENTS OF THE TWENTY-FIRST CENTURY—EVEN THOSE WHO ATTEND the few remaining one-room schools still found across the country—to imagine what schools might have been like one hundred plus years ago. Schools were furnished minimally, even sparsely, with simple wooden desks or benches where students sat with individual chalkboards (called "slates"), where the single teacher arrived early to build a fire

Students without shoes at a rural mountain school, circa 1930
COURTESY GAIL L. JENNER COLLECTION

in the wood stove or to set an urn of water with a single ladle near the door for drinking; new books were rarely seen; and students had to share books, paper and supplies, and often came to school barefoot or without proper clothing.

Indeed, there was a time in American history when almost every child who was not taught at home was educated in a small, often isolated, one-room school. These schools were initially governed by local entities, thus each school, including its furnishings, school materials and curriculum, even the quality of teaching, varied from one locale to another. Quite often, teachers had to rotate between schools because there were too few qualified teachers. Where winters were severe or pupils were needed at home, attendance was sporadic. Moreover, some districts required female teachers, if they were single, to leave their post if they married during the year. Many communities felt "schoolmarms" should remain single in order to teach effectively, and many young teachers were hardly older than their students.

President John Adams began his career as a teacher in a one-room school in Boston, and Abraham Lincoln was educated in a one-room schoolhouse—as were many of our other presidents and Founding Fathers. Many other influential Americans got their starts in one-room schools. Henry Ford loved his one-room school so much he eventually had it moved to a museum; award-winning author Joyce Carol Oates attended one in New York; Tony Hillerman, successful and noted author, attended Georgetown School in rural Oklahoma; and Laura Ingalls Wilder, whose family moved so often that she was not always able to attend school, began teaching in a one-room school at age fifteen. Her memories became the foundation for her stories and novels, and children of the 1970s and 1980s learned of a "typical" one-room schoolhouse through the television series *Little House on the Prairie*, which was based on Wilder's life and writings.

At the start of the twentieth century, at least half of American children were enrolled in the more than 210,000 one-room schools found across the nation. Whether they were made of stone or logs, sod or planks, these facilities became the heart of most communities, especially in the West where neighbors were separated by miles of prairie or tucked into isolated valleys. After World War I, however, many of these schools began to close. Migration away from the country and into cities minimized the need for so many schools; the trend toward consolidation had begun.

Today there are still as many as 400 operational one-room schools in the United States, mostly in rural areas. And more than 75 percent of them are in the states of Nebraska, Montana, South Dakota, California, and Wyoming.

Students gather at the Hooperville School in northern California, circa 1870s and 1880s

Early Education in America

President Thomas Jefferson believed that free public education was necessary to support a democracy; he wrote that a country populated by immigrants with different languages and traditions had to become educated in the traditions of a free democratic society in order to prepare them for self-government. Jefferson also stated that citizens of the new United States must be "literate, informed, and prudent." But the American concept of free and/or public schools actually began during colonial times.

Of all the colonies, Massachusetts became the first to pursue a number of educational innovations. In 1635, the first Latin Grammar School was established in Boston, Massachusetts; it was dedicated to teaching young men from upper classes. In Cambridge (then known as Newtowne), Massachusetts, Harvard College became the first university on American soil. It was founded in 1636. And in 1647, Massachusetts passed the Old Deluder Satan Act, which ruled that every town with fifty families or more must hire a schoolmaster. In addition, towns with one hundred families were required to hire a Latin grammar schoolmaster who could prepare the town's students for entrance into Harvard.

Interest in public education in the colonies wasn't exclusive to New England. In the South, Virginia became the site of the first actual "free school" in 1636. In South Carolina, the first publicly funded library was established in 1698. In 1727, Sisters of the Order of Saint Ursula in New Orleans sponsored a school for girls; it remains "the oldest continuously operating school for girls and the oldest Catholic school in the United States."

After the colonies won their independence from Great Britain, educational opportunities diversified and spread. Benjamin Franklin helped establish an "English Academy" in Philadelphia, with courses like history, geography, navigation, and foreign languages. The academy eventually became the University of Pennsylvania, and in 1787, the Young Ladies Academy opened in Philadelphia and became the first school for girls anywhere in the original thirteen colonies (now states).

The first permanent school for the deaf dates to 1817, the first for the blind to 1829—both were New England institutions. And in the 1830s, Horace Mann began to work in Massachusetts for an increase in free education and funding for public schools. In an attempt to prepare young teachers, in 1839, Massachusetts created the first state-funded school for teachers, later referred to as a "Normal" school. This was an important step in standardizing what teachers needed to know for teaching in schools throughout the state. As a result, other states began to establish Normal schools, and standardization in many areas of education began to spread.

A Short Glossary of Terms
Unfamiliar to Modern Readers

Blab school: a school where many lessons were conducted orally, where students recited aloud.

By Subscription: a means of paying for schools and teachers. Families "subscribed" to the school.

Ciphering: term used for basic math skills, e.g., adding and subtracting.

Common schools: used to denote public schools, funded by taxpayer money.

Deportment: behavior, used when grading students' behavior. Good deportment was an important component of public education.

Hornbook or Crib Book: a lesson printed on horn or another hard substance carried with students to and from school.

Normal School: an early type of secondary school, much like a junior college, where students were trained to be teachers. Generally these schools offered only two-year programs.

Primer: the first standardized schoolbook used in classrooms in the East and then brought to the West.

Reader: another term for primer.

Slate: a small hand-held blackboard used with a slate pencil for exercises, especially in places where paper was scarce and expensive.

Teacherage: a one-room school with teachers' quarters attached, commonly found in rural states like Montana.

Vernacular: native, "colloquial," based on local customs and/or traditions. In building traditions, vernacular or "folk vernacular" implies using local materials.

Texts and Textbooks

Repetition and recitation were common learning models in Colonial America, partly because of the rarity of printed materials. Lessons were carried via crib books or "hornbooks." These were little more than wooden paddles upon which a sheet of vellum was placed and lessons involving letters of the alphabet and/or a text from the Bible were inscribed.

Students were required to memorize their lessons and recite out loud. Here is one example of how a student might learn to read and recite important moral lessons, while learning the alphabet:

A—In Adam's Fall
    We sinned all.
B—Heaven to find,
    The Bible Mind.
C—Christ crucify'd
    For sinners dy'd.
D—The Deluge drown'd
    The Earth around.
E—Elijah hid
    By Ravens fed.
F—The judgment made
    Felix afraid.
G—As runs the Glass,
    Our Life doth pass.
H—My Book and Heart
    Must never part.
J—Job feels the Rod,
    Yet blesses GOD.

K—Proud Korah's troop
    Was swallowed up.
L—Lor fled to Zoar,
    Saw Fiery Shower
    On Sodom pour.
M—Moses was he
    Who Israel's Host
    Led thro' the Sea.
N—Noah did view
    The old world & new.
O—Young Obadias,
    David, Josias
    All were pious.
P—Peter deny'd
    His Lord and cry'd.
Q—Queen Esther sues
    And saves the Jews.

R—Young pious Ruth,
Left all for Truth.
S—Young Sam'l dear
The Lord did fear.
T—Young Timothy
Learnt sin to fly.
V—Vasthi for Pride,
Was set aside.

W—Whales in the Sea
GOD's Voice obey.
X—Xerxes did die,
And so must I.
Y—While youth so clear
Death may be near.
Z—Zaccheus he
Did climb the Tree
Our Lord to see.

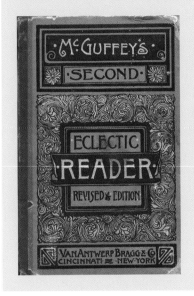

In 1690, Benjamin Harris printed the first *New England Primer* in Boston. Harris, who had emigrated from England, had produced a similar schoolbook in London.

The Primer quickly became the standard schoolbook for most New England students, with almost five million copies sold. *The Primer* also became known as the "Little Bible of New England" and was the forerunner to a number of readers used across the nation, including the *McGuffey Reader*, which would be found in schools all over America by the end of the nineteenth century.

McGuffey Readers were popular. This one dates to 1879.

The Three "Rs" in One Room

As Americans began to settle the West in the mid-nineteenth century, emigrants hoped to bring education with them. However, homesteads were often miles apart and towns only sprang up where enough trade or commerce provided a reason for their existence. Many settlements disappeared as quickly as they appeared, and transient populations meant fluctuating numbers of people to build, attend, and support schools. Because of the limitations, the number one answer to the question of how to educate the young continued to be the one-room schoolhouse model that had been well established in the East.

Each school was a world in and of itself and reflected the community in which it grew. In Oklahoma and other remote locations where conventional materials were hard to come by, for example, sod homes and schools were commonplace. Other rustic forms of construction included logs, clapboard or board-and-batten, adobe or stucco. Rarely was a wood frame or brick or stone building affordable in the earliest days of settlement.

In addition to their primitive nature, rural schools rarely stayed open nine months of the year. Generally, there were two terms based on both the ability of students to get to school and their parents' need for them on their homesteads. The summer term generally spanned the first of May through August, while the winter term spanned November through April. Older boys were often needed in the fields during spring planting or summer and fall harvest, and they could only attend school intermittently, most often during the winter months.

While the summer term might be stiflingly hot in the poorly ventilated buildings, the winter term was probably the hardest on children and their teachers. With freezing temperatures, only students closest to the schoolroom's single, pot-bellied stove stayed warm, so keeping an entire classroom warm became a full-time job. Families being served by a school were often required to contribute to the woodpile or coal supply.

Sod schools, like sod houses, offered few amenities.
COURTESY LIBRARY OF CONGRESS

The first Grand Junction School in Colorado
COURTESY GAIL L. JENNER COLLECTION

Two children heading to school in spite of the snow
COURTESY GAIL L. JENNER COLLECTION

Even then, students had to bundle up in heavy wool clothing, which often caused little bodies to itch and squirm.

At the Minersville School, a small schoolhouse located along the Trinity River in Trinity County, California, the new young teacher, Miss Shields—helped by the local miners who lived nearby—had to use "a sled pulled by horses to get the wood down to the school, and they stored it under the building. Then the boys split it in the morning and kept the wood box filled."

Weather was rarely a reason to miss school, unless conditions made travel absolutely impossible, and then those schools took a long winter break and resumed in the spring.

Even in more seasonable weather, merely getting to and from school was often a challenge in rural areas, for both students and teachers. Even into the twentieth century in some places, terrain, weather, and distance affected travel. Most children had to walk to school; if they were fortunate enough to have a horse, they rode.

George Leffingwell, a student at Brackett Creek School in Park County, Montana, in the 1940s, wrote: "We all rode horses to school and brought our own hay. One family had a five-mile ride to get to school by 9 a.m. Horse racing to and from school was prohibited. However, there was a one-mile stretch out of sight of both school and home, where all kinds of things would happen—from roping another horse's hind feet to getting a horse to buck by putting snowballs under its tail."

Another reminiscence comes from a woman named Sarah Secrest, who shared that her mother attended a one-room school in southwest Missouri where Secrest's grandfather was the bus driver. She doesn't know if the school was torn down or still stands, but she notes, "Schools in this area were built about five miles apart so students never had to walk more than two and a half miles to school, especially when weather was bad or other conditions kept the children at home. After grade eight they were either finished with their schooling, or they had to board in town to go to high school."

The school day often went from 9:00 a.m. to 4:00 p.m., and children also had chores to do before leaving for school or returning from school, so days were long. For rural children everywhere, life was composed of adult-like responsibilities, thus education often came in fragmented bits of time. Education for girls was considered far less important than for boys, and many never achieved more than a rudimentary education before marrying or settling down.

A retired naval officer, Norm Malmberg, told the story of his schooling:

I was raised on an Iowa farm, and I walked a mile to the nearby Goldenrod School. When I was five years old we moved two and a half miles to the family homestead. My grandparents who had been living there moved to Essex, Iowa, five miles away, so my parents took over farming their 160 acres, assisted by my grandparents, so then I walked one and a half miles to school. I had a younger sister and an older brother and we each had chores. My duties included tending the garden, about half an acre. I also tended the flock of three hundred laying hens. Each week we took five to thirty dozen egg cases and ten gallons of cream after hand-milking five to eight Holstein milk cows to town. We raised about one hundred pigs for butchering and sold beef from the milk cows' calves. We fed the pigs a mixture of buttermilk and grain and carried it in buckets to the feed trough.

In winter we often had one to four feet of snow, which had to be scooped away for feeding livestock. Then, when weather permitted, we shoveled animal manure from the feeding areas into our manure spreader for transfer to the fields.

At small rural schools, everyone knew everyone else. Jolyn Young wrote of her time in the one-room Bogus Elementary School near the Oregon-California border: "[Our] small school fostered a family atmosphere, with older kids helping younger ones and the teacher and aide knowing each child and their families. One drawback of a small student population was gathering up enough kids to make a full sports team. At the tender age of eight, I joined the volleyball team and competed against middle-school athletes from larger schools."

"Of course, we didn't have enough kids that were old enough at Bogus to make up our own team, so we joined forces with another small school to form a unique team. I was the smallest, and I was barely able to lob the ball over the net. I rolled up the waistband of my uniform shorts several times so they actually looked like shorts, but thanks to my pint-sized contributions, we had a team."

Others who talked about attending Bogus included Rose Atondo (whose children make up the sixth or seventh generation to attend Bogus) and Cicely Muelrath. Cicely remarked, "It was the best! Twenty-eight students, kindergarten through sixth grade. It was like one big family."

Peggy Germolis Denton wrote of her experience at Fiddletown School, "When I think of Fiddletown School, I think of *Little House on the Prairie.* All the kids were in the same class. . . . There is no way that you can sit there and not absorb, unless you completely plug your ears."

Mary Cowan wrote, "If anyone thinks we are in a wasteland just because we live in a rural area—this isn't true. . . . Being exposed to all the curriculum [sic], all the different people, all the different ages—[we were] more like a family, as my mother used to say. In a one-room school, it's more like a family instead of being in just with your own age group only."

Lois Kennedy, who celebrated her 103rd birthday in 2017, was born November 23, 1914, in Holman, Missouri, and had two half-sisters, both older. Her mother, who had emigrated from Germany as a young girl, and her father, a farmer, homesteaded in

Children at Bogus Elementary playing on the playground
COURTESY SISKIYOU COUNTY MUSEUM

eastern Colorado. When her father decided to become a minister the family lived near the churches he served in small towns throughout Nebraska.

When she was eighteen years old, Lois took her first job, teaching in a one-room school in Nebraska. Her time teaching was also her first year away from home, as she had to board in the home of the school board president and his family. And she still had to walk a half-mile to the school. Each day, as she'd exit the wire gate on the way out of the yard, a gaggle of geese would meet her and "escort" her down to the road, hissing all the way.

After she earned a small scholarship, Lois entered Doane College where she completed two years. Then she went to teach in a two-room school in Colfax, Nebraska.

Lois recalled, "Colfax was an interesting community with a number of immigrants." While there, she lived with a Czechoslovakian family and taught at the nearby school for two years. She then returned to Doane College where she was able to complete her degree in history and English.

Lois Kennedy's experience was exemplary of many of the dedicated teachers who served small communities all over the West. Laura Cowley's description of her first year of teaching, in 1920, was recorded in the 1989 *Siskiyou Pioneer*. She wrote,

> *I was scared and nervous. . . . It wasn't so bad. I loved all the kids. There were only about a dozen of them, mostly boys. They knew about me and I knew most of their parents. So it wasn't long until we had things going great. The kids took turns doing the janitor work. I hauled a can of water to school*

Miss Lois Kennedy as a student
COURTESY BEVERLY WENGER

every day. We all took our lunches. Someone supplied wood, and we made a fire in the old stove in the middle of the room when it was cold. We had programs and invited the neighborhood [and] everyone came. . . . By the end of the year, every child, from first grade to eighth, knew at least one hundred poems that they could recite any time.

Hardships were many for rural teachers, however. Mabel Townsley, who taught in South Dakota in 1899–1900, wrote in a letter to her friend Helen Myers:

When four o'clock comes, I have a romping game of tag with the children (which always makes me wonder at myself); split my kindling (and occasionally my thumb); sweep my dusty little room; close the shutters, lock the door, shoulder my dinner pail, and swing out. . . . When I reach home, I scrub for an hour in a room 8 degrees below zero, with hard, limey water. By this time, it is nearly suppertime. After this meal, where I eat enough for a man, there is only an hour and a half until bedtime (8:30).

The scene inside the classroom was quite different from today's modern schools, with two second grades, two third grades, and so on. Many of the early frontier schools were ungraded, and students were mixed and seated according to ability rather than strictly by age—though generally younger students were seated in front, older ones in back. Students were promoted to the next level when the teacher believed they were ready.

With everyone seated in one room, children were exposed to lessons many times over, which meant they often learned the lessons of their older companions. In addition, older students were often required to help younger ones so that the teacher was free to perform other duties.

In many frontier settlements, where even parents were illiterate, school lessons were often conducted orally. Children would repeat the teacher's oral lesson, in unison, at the top of their voices, especially if the school lacked books or other materials. Sometimes these schools became known as "blab" schools. Performing via memorization, or recitation, was prized and became a popular form of entertainment, as well as a learning tool, as parents came to listen to their children's lessons.

Along with recitation, reading, penmanship, and arithmetic were often considered the most important subjects and have been referred to as the "Three Rs" of education, that is, "Reading, 'Riting, and 'Rithmetic." "Ciphering," or arithmetic, was often practiced orally or on slates (small chalkboards). Since most one-room schools had few pencils and no paper, slates became a standard tool.

Boys with slates, from *In Picture-land*. McLoughlin Brothers. 1900.

William Hart's slate, from Little Shasta, California. Bell came from Emma Cramer, schoolteacher at Moffett Creek School, Scott Valley, California.
COURTESY VIRGINIA (GINNY) LAUSTALOT

Of course, deportment, or good behavior, was essential in schools. Teachers frequently punished students who did not abide by the rules. Discipline often included spanking—either by paddle or yardstick—or through humiliation. Sitting in a corner, with a dunce hat, or being made to sit outside, was not uncommon. Extra chores might also be required of the misbehaving student.

Grace Bennett of Siskiyou County, California, related that Chester Barton (born in 1891) once shared about Bill Kleaver's first day as teacher at the Riverside School on the Klamath River, circa 1910. "The big boys challenged him to a fight and he took them up on it. He came out fighting and had them all laid out on the floor with a few well-placed blows. The rest of the term was respectful and orderly!" Bill Kleaver later became county superintendent of Siskiyou County Schools.

Lee Craig, who attended a one-room school, wrote:

Our teachers had way more than they could do, so kids who bent, twisted, or broke the rules, were invited to stay after school and help. One wall was all blackboard and used for math problems, spelling words, or lists of assignments. The lucky student staying after school had the honor of washing the boards and taking out the erasers to hit them together and knock out all the chalk dust.

The next fun task was to move all the desks, then remove from a large barrel, something that looked like redwood sawdust with a slightly oily substance in it. The mixture was spread on the hardwood floor then swept up again. Afterward the desks were returned to their proper places in the proper rows. It is my understanding that they sometimes got them mixed up and students had to look for their desks the next morning.

After cleaning the floors, the offending student had to bring in wood for the stove (if it was winter), or wash the windows (if it was warm). On occasion, the restrooms needed cleaning as well. It wasn't too hard for the parents to find out how you did at school. If you came home late with white chalky arms and red hands, "the cat was out of the bag." What happened at school with the teacher was nothing compared to what happened after arriving home late. The teacher was an "extension" of the parenting process, so if you were in trouble at school, you were in trouble at home.

Elaine Zorbas's book, *Fiddletown Schoolhouse Memories*, included several amusing incidents collected from the school. Former student Mitch Lubenko wrote, "If there was any trouble, the teachers took care of it or got to your parents and you didn't want that. The

Little girl seated for misbehaving
COURTESY GAIL L. JENNER COLLECTION

teachers could spank you. They weren't scared; they had permission from your parents. That was it! You knew what you could get away with."

The teachers who held posts in these schools were critical to their communities and always remembered by their students—the good and the bad.

Schoolteacher Stories

And I am firm in my belief that a teacher lives on and on through his students. I will live if my teaching is inspirational, good, and stands firm for good values and character training. Tell me how can good teaching ever die? Good teaching is forever and the teacher is immortal.

—Jesse Stuart, American educator, 1958

Early schoolmasters or "schoolmarms" were required to do more than just teach. They were seen as role models, expected to be at Sunday service without fail, to sing in the church choir, and to teach music lessons in and out of school. They were expected to reach out to needy families, but most importantly, they were expected to maintain the schoolhouse and its grounds, including any cleaning or necessary repairs, even securing wood (or coal) for the all-important stove.

Rules were common, and lists of rules such as those on page 20 were generally agreed upon as part of a teacher's contract in schools around the West.

As families pushed west and homesteaded land, women, particularly single women over the age of twenty-five, were encouraged to travel west to teach, and a good number traveled from New England or the East Coast to small schools throughout the West, becoming the inspiration for the image of the old-fashioned schoolmarm on the prairie. Horace Mann, who became secretary of the Massachusetts State Board of Education in 1837, was a strong proponent of free education and worked for increased funding for public schools. In addition, he pursued better training for teachers. He also considered women to be potentially stronger teachers than their male counterparts. He believed "females are incomparably better teachers for young children than males. . . . Their manners are more mild and gentle, and hence in consonance with the tenderness of childhood."

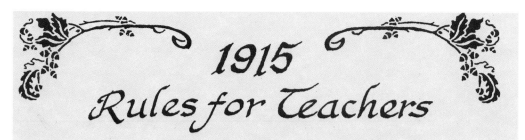

1915
Rules for Teachers

1. You will not marry during the term of your contract.

2. You are not to keep company with men.

3. You must be home between the hours of 8 p.m. and 6 a.m. unless attending a school function.

4. You may not loiter downtown in ice cream stores.

5. You may not travel beyond the city limits unless you have the permission of the chairman of the board.

6. You may not ride in a carriage or automobile with any man unless he is your father or brother.

7. You may not smoke cigarettes.

8. You may not dress in bright colors.

9. You may under no circumstances dye your hair.

10. You must wear at least two petticoats.

11. Your dresses must not be any shorter than two inches above the ankle.

12. To keep the school room neat and clean, you must: sweep the floor at least once daily, scrub the floor at least once a week with hot, soapy water, clean the blackboards at least once a day, and start the fire at 7 a.m. so the room will be warm by 8 a.m.

Old Sacramento Schoolhouse Museum

List of rules for teachers, circa 1915

However, that opinion did not win out in every area. In 1871, 52 percent of all teachers in Nebraska were men; in Kansas, 47.2 percent were men.

Elsie Petsel Hallock of Ainsworth, Nebraska, wrote in the late 1800s of her choice to start a career in education: "In my hometown, the only highly respectable jobs for girls after they graduated from high school were nursing, teaching or clerking in a store.... by the time I'd completed my normal training in high school I [was] still be too young to go into nurse's training, [but] I was going to be respectable and was going to earn a living. So, I became a teacher."

For some women, the choice was not always one that turned out exactly as they had hoped. Maude Frazier, a teacher in Nevada, wrote in her memoir *Maude Frazier: Nevadan*: "It is quite possible that it was never intended by the good Lord that I should be a schoolteacher. At least not so soon after the turn of the Twentieth Century, when they [students] were definitely a distinct species.... Early in the 1900s, women teachers suffered most of the restrictions of nuns, with none of the advantages they enjoyed.... Nobody defined exactly what a teacher's place was, but everyone knew she should keep it."

In rural areas, teachers often had to board with the families served by the local school. Board and room were commonly considered part of the teacher's salary—which was generally minimal, at best. Elisabeth Langdon Doggett, who was hired in 1913 to teach at Forks of Salmon School in northern California, lived at the old hotel, a building with no inside plumbing or water, for her first year at the school. Her only light was a kerosene lamp. For her second year, she was moved to a small cabin across from the graveyard.

In 1915, Miss Irene Yank, who taught at Kenyon School in Shasta County in northern California, boarded at the Baker ranch until winter storms made it impossible to cross the swollen creek to get to the school. Mr. Baker then constructed a small house near the school where his own daughters and Miss Yank could stay during the winter. Later on a larger "teacherage" was built: a small, two-story house with a screened-in porch across the front. A number of teachers used these quarters until they fell into disrepair, especially after some local goats were penned up inside the porch—as a prank. The teacherage was later sold and removed from the premises.

Some teachers in more remote regions had to actually pack in weekly, biweekly, or even monthly to reach their schools. One such schoolteacher was Miss Leona Lewis Bryan. She packed into the Junction School at Somes Bar, Siskiyou County, California, in March 1928. According to the 1989 issue of *The Siskiyou Pioneer*, Miss Bryan was "led by Ralph and Gil Smith, owners of the pack train, which also delivered the mail. School was operated March through November to accommodate harsh winter weather and was

Minnie Smith's first teaching assignment at Forks of Salmon School
COURTESY GAIL L. JENNER COLLECTION

termed 'Summer School, grades 1–8.' Leona lived in a small one-room cabin. Her first salary was $1600.00 in 1928."

Miss Minerva Starritt also had to pack into the mountains and the trip often took more than a day. She wrote that she taught seven years "on the Klamath [River]. . . . I was no stranger to the district. I knew the people and the children." In 1935, "When school opened in September, I had fifty-two children and all eight grades."

Most communities stepped in to help teachers get prepared when necessary. Miss Starritt wrote about several who assisted her. For example, they came to help her clear off a hillside to build a playground, and even the state road crew did their part.

One student's father was an excellent pianist and came to school twice a week in the afternoons to help with music. As she noted, "School programs were important. . . . The entire community far and wide would come to the school plays and games." One event, however, did not go quite as planned! "We were preparing a gala for Christmas. . . . We had built a stage at the end of the room, six inches off the floor and put candle footlights on the stage. I was wearing a long white polka dot dress. In the middle of the program, I was standing too close to one of the footlights, and my dress caught fire. . . . one of the parents grabbed me and put the fire out. The show went on."

Vella Munn, successful author of more than forty historical novels, shared what it was like for her mother, a one-room school teacher at Washington Bar School in northern California: "My mother, a single parent, had been hired to teach the 16 to 17 students in the local one-room schoolhouse."

Washington Bar School, where Vella Munn's mother and grandmother taught
COURTESY VELLA MUNN

Washington Bar came into being in 1849 during California's gold rush. Proof of hydraulic mining still scars several mountainsides while the countless boulders at the river's edge serve as testament to the Chinese who tried to make a living there. The last time I was in Washington the woman who owned the grocery store told me several miners still pay for their groceries in gold dust. When my family lived there, logging kept the town alive. These days the hotel and recreational opportunities do the same.

At seven I had little interest in what being the only single woman and only college educated person in town was like for Mother. What mattered was that everyone knew my sister and me. . . . Give us a deer trail to follow or tree to climb. There was no such thing as a babysitter, and although at first my sister was too young for school, Mother brought her along.

One day I was sick so we both stayed home, caring for and bedeviling each other. Our little house (it had been a shed before the owner remodeled it so the teacher would have a roof over her head) was heated with a wood stove. My sister tried to pick up the lid for the opening through which wood was fed, and of course, burned herself. I filled the kitchen sink with cold water, and my sister kept her hand in it until Mother got home. We were hoping to keep the mishap to ourselves but my sister's blistered palm and tears gave her away.

There was no TV or radio reception and no newspapers. The world didn't concern us. My sister and I were only marginally aware of how drafty the school building was, how cold in winter (Mother was responsible for keeping the wood stove going) or how stuffy it became as the days warmed.

My sister and I lived a life of perpetual present. We believed we'd always live in Washington shut off from the world we cared little about, but it wasn't to be. After two and a half years there, Mother's contract wasn't renewed. We had to leave. Of course we went with her—to Lime Kiln, a nearby farming/ranching community. Again she was the only teacher and taught all eight grades in a single classroom. I graduated from the eighth grade with two others and went off to that scary-big Nevada City high school.

In *Rifle Reveille*, a weekly newspaper published in Rifle, Colorado, the following was written by a schoolteacher about [her] students in 1896:

The class work is showing more and more those who are earnest about their education, those who have a determined purpose to get all there is to be gotten out of a year's school work, and those who are careless seemingly, or do not desire to benefit themselves with these opportunities so freely offered. These nice spring days require an effort for boys to tear themselves away from their tops and horseshoes. Yet he who does so conquers in manhood, and yes in womanhood, too, for in the intellectual realm man has found his peer in woman.

For many early schoolteachers, exposing students to new experiences was an important element in their teaching. In 1923, Miss Mary E. Dickey, a teacher at the Kenyon School in Shasta County, California, decided to take her students to the fair in Sacramento, approximately 160 miles south. Parents agreed to the trip, and a group of six adults and nine children set out in September. Mr. Kuney was selected to drive Mr. Bibbens' open-sided car.

Unimproved roads made travel slow, and when a tire went flat, the children piled out to explore their surroundings while the tire was being repaired. Miss Dickey recognized that every experience on this journey south was likely a new one so she let them explore. One of their discoveries turned out to be a nearby electric railroad line (built in 1910). Hastening to catch up, she was relieved when a fence kept the children from getting too close.

At last, Miss Dickey and her troupe reached Sacramento. While the parents of the younger students found a place to camp for the night, Miss Dickey took the two eldest students—two eighth graders, Elsie Bibbens and Nolan Pehrson—to a private home where she was able to rent rooms.

The next day the students and chaperones went to the fair where they were greeted by an old miner and his donkey. They also toured the state Capitol building and historic Sutter's Fort. As a graduation present, Miss Dickey took Elsie and Nolan to a restaurant for lunch.

In gratitude, Mrs. Pehrson (in whose home Miss Dickey boarded) deducted $20 from the teacher's next month's room and board, which normally cost Miss Dickey $40 a month.

Leslie Ralston shared that her mother, who was born in Broken Bow, Nebraska, spent time with her great aunt who was a schoolteacher at two Nebraska rural schools in the early twentieth century, one at Round Valley and one at Snake Run. "My mom would stay with Aunt Faye for a few months at a time, and she and Aunt Faye would ride to school. Aunt Faye had a big gray horse while Mom had a pony named Buster and one named Trixie. Every day they rode to school—even in the snow—but one year they had a blizzard blow in, and Uncle Loren had to go and look for them with his plow team because the snow got so deep!"

Teachers were fortunate if they had the opportunity to pursue further educational courses or workshops. The rise of various "teachers institutes" was one way that schoolteachers could meet and learn from each other, as well as learn about what was happening in the field of education. But getting to the institutes was not always easy.

In the fall of 1913, six instructors from Weaverville, Trinity County, California, left to attend the annual teachers institute on the coast, in Eureka, California. According to one instructor,

> *Their transportation was an open five-passenger touring car. At that time there was no road to Eureka down the main Trinity River, only the newly opened Red Bluff road to the coast. The route took them through Douglas City, Hayfork, Peanut, Auto Rest (later, Forest Glen), Cobb, Dinsmores, and Bridgeville.*
>
> *It took the travelers three days to reach Eureka. The closing event of the institute was a banquet, and they arrived just in time to attend the banquet. Those present stood up and cheered as the teachers entered the dining hall. After eating and signing the*

Several young people from Scott Valley, California, ride in an open touring car similar to one in which the Weaverville teachers rode to the coast.
COURTESY JENNER FAMILY COLLECTION

attendance roster so that their pay would not be docked, the group had to turn right around and head back to Weaverville via the same tedious route. Thankfully the return trip only took them two days.

The entire trip was marked by 22 blowouts, flats, and breakdowns! While thus halted, those not actually engaged in repair work spread a rug on the ground and played cards. . . . The little party stayed overnight at Bridgeville, but found only two beds available. The three ladies slept in one of the beds, the three men in the other. The latter found it more comfortable to sleep crosswise in their bed.

Everett Conroy, a former student shared a humorous memory from his days at Humbug School in Siskiyou County, California, where his teacher was Mr. Walter Creed. He wrote, "He was quite elderly and would drop off to sleep. One day they took off his glasses and put dots of colored crayon on them." One can only imagine what happened when Mr. Creed awoke!

Humbug School children
COURTESY PERRY SIMS

ONE ROOM

Perhaps Mary Abigail Dodge, who wrote *Our Common Schools* in 1880, said it best when she wrote the following poem about life as a teacher of the one-room school:

'Twas Saturday night, and a teacher sat
Alone, her task pursuing:
She averaged this and she averaged that
Of all her class were doing.
She reckoned percentage, so many boys,
And so many girls all counted,
And marked all the tardy and absentees,
And to what all the absence amounted.

Names and residence wrote in full,
Over many columns and page;
Yankee, Teutonic, African, Celt,
And averaged all their ages,
The date of admission of every one,
And cases of flagellation,
And prepared a list of the graduates
For the coming examination.

Her weary head sank low on her book,
And her weary heart still lower,
For some of her pupils had little brain
And she could not furnish more.
She slept, she dream; it seemed she died,
And her spirit went to Hades,
And they met her there with a question fair,
"State what the per cent of your grade is."

Ages had slowly rolled away,
Leaving but partial traces.
And the teacher's spirit walked one day
In the old familiar places.
A mound of fossilized school reports
Attracted her observation,
As high as the State House Dome, and as wide
As Boston since annexation.

> She came to the spot where they buried her bones,
>   And the ground was well built over,
> But laborers digging threw out a skull
>   Once planted beneath the clover.
> A disciple of Galen wandering by,
>   Paused to look at the diggers,
> And plucking the skull up, looked through the eye,
>   And saw it was lined with figures.
>
> "Just as I thought," said the young M.D.,
>   "How easy it is to kill 'em—"
> Statistics ossified every fold
>   Of cerebrum and cerebellum.
> "It's a great curiosity, sure," said Pat,
>   "By the bones can you tell the creature?"
> "Oh, nothing strange," said the doctor, "that
>   Was a nineteenth century teacher."

Mary Jensen shared that her grandmother, Margaret Ott, who was born on December 29, 1906, in Geddes, South Dakota, attended Chillicothe Ohio Teachers' College. "The one or possibly two-year program certified her as a teacher in South Dakota for all grade levels, first through twelfth grades. . . . [She] was the first in the Ott family to attend any form of college."

After attending Teachers' College, Margaret got a job as the only teacher in a one-room schoolhouse in rural South Dakota. She was about nineteen years old, and it was not unusual for her to have pupils as tall or as old as she.

As the town's teacher, she lived with her pupils' families, rotating residences. Her job description included transporting pupils from distant farms and starting the fire each cold morning. She said those extra jobs were harder for her than planning lessons for all twelve grades. One story about Margaret was that on a particularly bad morning her car brakes failed as she drove up to a child's home. She (car and all) entered the family's breakfast nook!

Of course, there were moments that required a teacher to respond authoritatively. Oda Brown, who taught in the Midwest near the turn of the century, wrote about a few incidents: "One boy had to write one hundred sentences for making fun of the accent of a classmate's father who had immigrated from the Azores Islands as he drove his team of horses past the school."

In another incident, "Major Huey sneaked a lizard into the schoolhouse in his pocket at the end of recess one day and as soon as studies resumed and everyone became quiet, he dropped the squirming reptile down the back of Emily Robert's dress. She let out a shriek as she jumped straight out of her seat, then started peeling off her clothes as she raced for the door!"

One can only imagine what that teacher said to young Major Huey.

Of course, there were pranks that didn't always bring about a harsh punishment from the teachers.

Delbert Glavich shared a story in *Fiddletown Schoolhouse Memories*: "We had skunks in [a] trap and put them under the schoolhouse and she [Miss DeCartret] had to let school out, it stunk so bad. They sent us to the Trustees and they just laughed at us. 'You guys know better than that. Don't do it next time. Get out of here!'" And, Delbert also wrote, "We tipped the girls' toilet over a lot of times on Halloween!"

Lester E. Newton taught at the Rocky Mountain School in Humboldt County, California, from late August 1936 through May of 1938. He wrote, "There were about twenty students enrolled each year, but there was quite a turnover during the year because of parents leaving to work at jobs in other areas and new parents moving into any available homes . . . Over one-half of the students were cousins."

He continued, "During my first term, the opening day of deer season was on a Friday. After lunch on Thursday, two school board members and the husband of the third board member came in and announced that school was to be dismissed [that day] at 1:30, so that those who wanted to go hunting [could] leave."

Several decades later, Jeri Christopher, who now lives in Nevada, wrote about her first year of teaching in an isolated rural school in Oregon: "As a first-year teacher in the 1980s, I found myself on the threshold of a one-room schoolhouse and a treasured experience in eastern Oregon. I was to be the teacher of seven little 'buckaroo' kids. It had been a year since the school had had a certified teacher; the last one had quit during the previous year, and she had been replaced by a local ranch girl."

She described her encounter with her new charges, the oldest of whom was a twelve-year-old boy who promptly informed her that "our last teacher started crying and smoking cigarettes. . . . What are you gonna do?"

This "buckaroo" was "closely shadowed by his blonde-haired, meek and mild sister, a second grader. And she was being trailed by a spirited, curly-headed plump little kindergarten girl . . . also a kindergarten girl arrived by car, brought in by her mama from an outlying ranch. The last two were my own two sons, a second grader and a four year old . . . [and] of course, I can't forget our faithful friend, Brownie, who settled himself on our front porch and barked each day at 3:00, reminding us to go home because school had been over for half an hour."

As Jeri came to learn, "the only one who knew the alphabet was my own son," but she was determined to tackle this and other curriculum problems. For example, for her social studies lessons, she found "stored away in the back of a dark, dusty, forgotten closet, an old set of maps. Each day we would put the maps on the floor and gather 'round. Being a history buff, and being guided by the progression of the maps, I told them stories of the past." The kids quickly began to appreciate the world stretching out in front of them.

In the end, Ms. Christopher stayed for four more "equally great years and many more precious memories!"

In Luther Bryan Clegg's collection of schoolhouse memories from Texas students and teachers, titled *The Empty Schoolhouse*, Louise Smith Callan shared, "I taught the older children, and my twin sister Lois taught the younger ones. . . . We had to decide who was going to be the principal. The principal automatically made ten dollars more. I taught the older children so I got the hundred dollars and Lois got the ninety dollars. Then we split that extra ten dollars. Even though I was called principal, we worked together, but I was more or less responsible for getting reports ready and turning them in." She went on to write, "We had to walk about a mile to school. The older boys built the fires; someone was always there and had the fires built. They did all the extra chores and everything for us. There was a cistern. We drew that water out of there with a bucket. We had a happy time out there."

Another Texas teacher, Picola Foreman, wrote about her experiences teaching at Salt Creek in Stonewall County, Texas, in 1925.

I was about twenty-four when I taught there. I was expected to live in the community, because I had no other choice. . . . I had about twelve students and stayed with a family that was just a half-mile from school. . . . Most of the kids brought their lunch and hung 'em on the old heater to keep them warm. They all had sausage and biscuits and maybe fruit, if they could afford it. Most of the kids would go barefooted in the spring by choice. They had shoes. They were ranch people. . . . The school building was set on rocks. . . . Those men didn't close them in around the sides, and lots of times there'd be skunks under there and snakes—rattlesnakes. One time I took the kids down to a little gully for a little picnic, and that very evening, the man I stayed with came back with a big rattler he killed down there. We watched closely, and nobody was ever bitten by a rattler while I was there.

Such were the vagaries of teaching in remote and outlying areas of the West.

Moving West

FROM THE DISTANCE OF A HUNDRED AND FIFTY YEARS, THE SETTLEMENT OF THE WEST in the United States looks like another inevitable step in the Manifest Destiny of the growing country. But many factors played into the spread of citizens into the territories west of the Mississippi River. And those factors also influenced the educational systems of the West.

Perhaps the greatest influencer of the earliest waves of settlement was the discovery of gold in California after the Mexican-American War opened up that territory for American settlement. Probably the second greatest influencer in the development of the West, however, was the Homestead Act of 1862, signed into law by President Lincoln in the early years of the Civil War. Prior to the Homestead Act, anyone hoping to purchase lands in the West owned by the federal government had to buy at least 320 acres of the unsettled land, at $1.25 per acre. According to the National Archives, "The investment needed to purchase these large plots and the massive amount of physical labor required to clear the land for agriculture were often insurmountable obstacles."

A homestead bill that would eliminate much of the land speculation and make the development of homesteads more affordable had been promoted and passed by the House of Representatives in 1858 but was defeated by the Senate. In 1859, a second homestead bill passed both houses but was vetoed by President James Buchanan. Buchanan, often considered one of America's worst presidents, believed that states and territories had a right to determine if they would allow slavery. He was not about to upset the balance of power between slave and non-slave states, therefore he was not about to promote settlement of the West since new anti-slavery states would elevate the issue dramatically.

In response to Buchanan's laissez-faire attitude, in 1860, Lincoln and his newly formed Republican Party platform included a plank advocating homestead legislation, and when it passed in 1862, the language approved by the thirty-seventh Congress allowed:

Clinton Custer and team plow, Oro Fino, California
COURTESY CLINT AND PAT CUSTER

That any person who is the head of a family, or who has arrived at the age of twenty-one years, and is a citizen of the United States, or who shall have filed his declaration of intention to become such, as required by the naturalization laws of the United States, and who has never borne arms against the United States Government or given aid and comfort to its enemies, shall, from and after the first January, eighteen hundred and sixty-three, be entitled to enter one quarter section or a less quantity of unappropriated public lands, upon which said person may have filed a preemption claim, or which may, at the time the application is made, be subject to preemption at one dollar and twenty-five cents, or less, per acre; or eighty acres or less of such unappropriated lands, at two dollars and fifty cents per acre, to be located in a body, in conformity to the legal subdivisions of the public lands, and after the same shall have been surveyed: Provided, That any person owning and residing on land may, under the provisions of this act, enter other land lying contiguous to his or her said land, which shall not, with the land so already owned and occupied, exceed in the aggregate one hundred and sixty acres.

The legislation had a huge impact. By the end of the Civil War, fifteen thousand homestead claims had been filed, and more settlement followed in the postwar years. Women made a number of the homestead claims. Eventually, 1.6 million claims were approved. The Homestead Act transformed America's landscape and introduced settlement from the plains to the coastal regions of America. The Act remained in effect for more than one hundred years; the final claim, filed for 80 acres in Alaska, was approved in 1988.

Immigration also impacted the settlement of the West as eastern cities and states became more crowded and new arrivals came, seeking economic opportunity. Over a million Irish immigrants arrived in the United States in the 1840s because of the potato famine. And from 1870 to 1890, nearly sixteen million immigrants flooded into the United States. Immigrants settled at least fifty-eight counties in Kansas. In 1890, in North Dakota, 43 percent of the population was foreign-born. And in Wyoming, one out of seven arrivals was an immigrant. By 1900, 47.6 percent of the total population in eleven western states was composed of immigrants.

ALASKA

Discussion regarding the purchase of Alaska from Russia paralleled the westward expansion of the United States. In 1864–67, the Western Union Telegraph Expedition to Alaska brought attention to the region. In a speech Charles Sumner gave to the United States Senate, he stated that Russia "wished to strip herself of all outlying possessions as Napoleon had stripped himself of Louisiana, in order to gather her strength for her struggle with England for the Control of Asia."

Many would wonder why Alaska, but as the tide of nationalism and expansionism took hold, the decision to purchase Alaska was probably inevitable. The United States purchased the territory in 1867.

When gold was discovered in the Canadian Klondike in 1897, the rush was on. Prospectors arrived by the tens of thousands and these men were responsible for blazing trails into the interior.

In the wake of the gold rush came a more serious look at the Alaskan frontier. According to the census, by 1929, the population of Alaska was 59,278, but that figure was actually based on estimates of the Native populations by priests and missionaries and local records. Their full numbers will probably never be known.

According to the 1930 census, of the 28,640 whites in Alaska, only 10,990 had been born in the United States, of American parents; either the mother or father, or both, of approximately 7,470 had been foreign born, and more than 10,000 were born in foreign countries themselves; 6,359 of these were naturalized American citizens. Finally, Alaskan residents who were either immigrants or the children of immigrants totaled

Miners and their family in Alaska, circa 1903

Life was hard for immigrant children, and an education was not easy to obtain.
COURTESY GAIL L. JENNER COLLECTION

17,650. Most of these came from Canada or northern Europe, e.g., Norway, Sweden, Germany, England, and Finland.

As described in the 1930 census, Alaska's Native population was divided into four groups, each inhabiting a different geographic region. The "original tribe of the southeast was considered to be the Tlingit," and they numbered 4,462. The second group included the Athapascan (or Tinneh) Indians and totaled 4,935.

The Aleuts—who are related to the Eskimos but are different in language and customs—made up the third group; however, they were combined with the Eskimos (the fourth group). Together their population totaled about 19,028 in 1930. Broken down, the Eskimos numbered about fifteen thousand and the Aleuts about four thousand.

Clearly Alaska became a melting pot of various groups. And since they were spread out across landscapes that were not easy to cross or settle, educating the children was a difficult task.

In 1915, Anchorage opened its first public school in its Pioneer Hall building (later known as Pioneer School). There were four teachers hired and over a hundred students enrolled. In 1917, a second school was established to handle the increasing student population, which totaled some 206 students.

It wasn't until 1939 that Anchorage opened its first high school, in addition to an elementary school and a 570-seat auditorium. It was funded by a $101,250 grant from the federal government and by a voter-approved bond. The school, designed by well-known architects Naramore & Naramore, was so well constructed it survived the 1964 Alaska earthquake with no damage.

More important, the "Native question" was, as in other parts of the West, subject to the prevailing attitudes of the time as well as changing and confusing federal regulations and policies.

In 2003, Cheryl Easley, PhD, and others conducted research as part of a "Voices of our Elders" project, funded by the US Department of Health and Human Services through the Administration on Aging. As outlined in her paper *Boarding School: Historical Trauma among Alaska's Native People*, "The educational policies that took place in Alaska in the late 1800s and early 1900s were a continuation of US government policy that began in 1879 as a result of western expansion in the continental United States. These new policies focused on treaty-making that put Indians on reserves and educated Indian children in boarding schools."

Without question, the popular attitude of the time was that "it was easier to control an Indian with a hoe in his hand rather than with him on a horse, waving a rifle." Removing Indian children from their homes and installing them in boarding schools made it easier to assimilate them into the culture. Harsh, strict rules regarding language and other customs were enforced, often through corporal punishment.

While a number of missionary "day" schools had been introduced in Alaska in the decades prior to acquisition by the United States, boarding schools sponsored by the government were purported to offer the "best means" of bringing Native people into alignment with the general population.

One of the first schools built for the Tlingit people near Sitka was at Wrangell in 1877. In its first years, it was a mission and a day school. In 1878 it became a girls' school and remained open until 1889.

John G. Broday opened the Presbyterian Mission School in 1878, but in 1884 it was reopened as the first Sitka Industrial Training School; it taught carpentry, machinery courses, and carving for boys and later, courses for girls were introduced. Into the 1900s, the Mission School, along with the Roman Catholic Mission of the Holy Cross and a school at the reserve at Metlakatla, were the only schools open to Native children.

Eskimo school children, early 1900s
COURTESY GAIL L. JENNER COLLECTION

In 1884, the US Congress passed the Organic Act, requiring the Interior Department to provide education for all children in Alaska, without regard to race. Funding for schools increased from $25,000 to $40,000, but providing an education still proved difficult in the rugged regions of the territory.

Churches stepped in to open schools for Native students, while non-Native schools were established in Sitka, Juneau, and Douglas. Teachers were paid only $800 a year, less than teachers in the continental states.

In 1886, in his address to the US Congress, Sheldon Jackson, the General Agent of Education for Alaska, declared, "They [Native Alaskans] are savages, and with the exception of those in Southern Alaska, have not had civilizing, educational, or religious advantages. . . . They need to be taught both the law of God and the law of the land."

As the onslaught of thousands of prospectors overwhelmed the territory—many bringing their families—boomtowns sprang up, and many of them did build schools, but most of these eventually closed or were abandoned as miners moved on.

One of the most significant results of the gold rush was the introduction and spread of diseases that killed thousands of Native Alaskans, a period of time that has since been referred to as the time of "great deaths." The people died from cholera, diphtheria, influenza, smallpox, measles, venereal diseases, tuberculosis, and alcoholism.

As disease swept over the frozen frontier, thousands of Native children were orphaned or left homeless. In response, missionaries, as well as the government, established orphanages. At the same time, missionary schools were being replaced by boarding schools to be run by the Bureau of Indian Affairs (BIA). Finally, the 1884 Organic Act of Alaska was revised in 1912 to provide education to whites and Natives of "mixed blood who lead a civilized life in parts of the territory outside incorporated areas."

According to Jim La Belle's master's thesis, prepared for Dr. Easley, the former dean of the College of Health and Social Welfare at the University of Alaska Anchorage, "Many children were sent to places foreign to them. In many cases, kids from the plains were sent to mountainous and forest regions of the State. The Wrangell Institute Boarding School, deep in the heart of the Southeast Panhandle, was one such place. . . . Many would not understand why their parents would let them go. . . . The authorities came and loaded thousands of children from hundreds of villages across Alaska onto boats, skiffs, dog teams, and sleds for shipment to rural centers for redeployment to larger gathering places like Fairbanks and Anchorage. About 400 would go to Wrangell."

As part of the educational policy, children had to be taken away in order to discourage family visits. Again, Easley pointed out, "A cadre of BIA employees, Native and non-Native alike, would meet the aircraft coming in from rural centers. . . . From a roster, the employees would determine the names of the children (some as young as five years of age) and their village of origin and then tether them together by small pieces of rope. Sometimes a rope held a few kids, other times 10 to 15."

In 1932, the Wrangell Institute Boarding School was established on Wrangell Island in the Alaskan Panhandle. Wrangell had originally been founded by the Russians and was one of the oldest non-Native settlements in Alaska. The school remained in operation from 1932 to 1975.

Much has been written about the abuses and mistreatment of the Native children at Wrangell. Many returned home confused and bitter, unable to make the adjustment back to their family and culture. According to Easley, "The moral impacts of those bygone educational policies are evident today. There are many boarding school-era students who have faced a loss of cultural identity, language, and tradition. . . . Since the mid-1970s, these individuals have made up the high percentages of alcohol-fueled statistics. . . . They have been living on the margins of both societies, caught between the Native world and the Western world."

Recovery for many of these individuals has come about slowly. In 1993, the Episcopal Church became involved with Indigenous Healing, as addressed by Archbishop Michael

Peers of the Anglican Church of Canada. He wrote, "I accept and confess before God and you, our failures in the residential schools. We failed you. We failed ourselves. We failed God. I am sorry more than I can say: that we were a part of a system which took you and your children from home and family. . . that we tried to remake you in our image. . . . That in our schools so many were abused. On behalf of the Anglican Church of Canada, I offer our apology."

Alaska still has a number of successful one- or two-room schools. Labouchere Bay School in Labouchere Bay is located on Prince of Wales Island, the fourth largest island in the United States and the ninety-seventh largest island in the world. The island is the traditional home of the Tlingit, but miners arrived in the late nineteenth century and settled there, and, as logging became the island's dominant industry, the population grew and so did the need to educate the young.

In spite of its many failures, without these important outlying rural schools, Alaska's student population would suffer severely.

ARIZONA

The land that would become the Grand Canyon State in 1912 would not be widely settled until after World War II, but due to the discovery of copper in the state, the territory, which was originally part of New Mexico and became a separate territory in 1863, had sparse and transient settlements all over by the end of the nineteenth century.

The first European, Fray Marcos de Niza, had passed through what would become Lochiel, in Santa Cruz County, Arizona, around 1539. Located along the Mexican border, twenty-four miles east of Nogales, it became a mining town in the late nineteenth century. It had three saloons, a bakery, a stable, five stores, a mansion, a butcher shop, and a population of about four hundred people. Mexican revolutionary Pancho Villa often crossed the border here to steal cattle before slipping back to Mexico safely.

Today Lochiel is a ghost town, located on private property, but several buildings—including a church, the old U.S. Customs Station, and a one-room schoolhouse and teacherage—are visible from the road. Interestingly, several movies, including *Monte Walsh, Oklahoma!* and *Tom Horn*, were filmed here.

☖

Other preserved school buildings can be found around the state, as well. The Strawberry Schoolhouse is the oldest standing schoolhouse in Arizona. It is found in Gila County, in the northwest corner of Arizona. In 1884, settlers living in Strawberry Valley petitioned the county school superintendent for a school. The petition was granted, giving birth to District #33.

Arizona resident and artist Carolyn Sato recalled that the interior of the hand-hewn school was much lovelier than most pioneer schools. "Wainscoting reached from the floor to a height of four feet. Cloth was stretched and nailed above that and wallpaper was glued to the cloth." In addition, "glass windows were installed, two on the east side and two on the west. They were double-hung and could be raised and lowered. A bell hung over the door on the south side and a wood-burning stove sat in the middle of the room."

Story has it that a dispute over the school's proposed location, however, led to an unusual solution: using a rope, cowboys measured the distance between two homesteads, the Hicks-Duncan cabin to the west and the Peach cabin to the east. Halfway between the two they built the one-room log cabin schoolhouse.

After the Strawberry School was closed in 1916, the abandoned structure fell into disrepair. In 1961, it was sold to Fred Eldean, who gave it to the Payson-Pine Chamber of Commerce. Some restoration was done, but then, with the support of the Arizona Historical Society, the Pine/Strawberry Archeological and Historical Society managed to complete the restoration.

Mormon pioneers originally settled Mount Trumbull, Arizona. Mount Trumbull, for which the town was named, is about twelve miles away. The town was also known as "Bundyville," after one of the town's families. The town was originally established in 1916, and the current schoolhouse was built in 1922.

A one-room schoolhouse and a number of abandoned buildings plus a few other structures are all that remain of the town. The school was abandoned in the late 1960s, but restoration on some exterior and interior portions has begun.

After Geronimo and his men surrendered to the US Army, residents in and around Skeleton Canyon, Arizona, were eager for a schoolhouse. Geronimo (1829–1908), chief of the Chiricahua Apaches, had led his tribe against Arizona's white settlers for more than ten years. He surrendered in 1886, and he and his tribe were taken to Fort Sill, Oklahoma.

A schoolhouse of sorts opened in 1910, but with the purchase of land, in 1914, from Jane and J. J. Wheeler for $25.00, Apache Elementary School had a permanent home. The school continued to operate for over one hundred years with as few as one or two students or as many as twenty students. After graduating from the eighth grade, students transferred to Douglas, San Simon, or even Animas, New Mexico, to attend high school.

In spite of recent movements to close the school (because there were fewer than the "required" eight students), the parents and residents have fought to keep the school open. Located between the Peloncillo and Chiricahua Mountains, as of 2018, the Apache Elementary School District was one of four remaining one-room districts in Arizona.

Geronimo was a leader and medicine man from the Bedonkohe band of the Chiricahua Apache tribe.
WIKIMEDIA COMMONS

🔔

The Tubac School, in Pima County, Arizona, was established around 1876–77, after residents petitioned the superintendent of schools for a school. Mr. T. Lillie Mercer was the school's first schoolmaster, and thirty students were enrolled (including three of his children). The first classes were held at one end of the Otero General Store, and because so many of the children were of Mexican descent, lessons were taught in Spanish and English.

By 1885, there was a schoolhouse, funded by Mr. Sabino Otero, a rancher and prominent citizen. It was an adobe structure with a packed dirt floor. Mrs. Sarah Black was the first teacher. The school grew, in numbers of both pupils and teachers; by the 1890s, there were sometimes as many as 140 students and three instructors. Today, the Tubac School is an immersion school for visiting students and is run by the Tubac Presidio State Historic Park.

🔔

The Lehi School, in Mesa, Arizona, was built in 1913 and is the oldest standing school in Mesa today. The Rogers family provided land for the first school in the 1880s. It was a simple one-room adobe structure, but the community outgrew it and a new school was built in 1914. Today the school is also the site of the Mesa Historical Museum.

🔔

Valentine, Arizona, was the site of the former Truxton Canyon Training School, a reservation boarding school established to teach primarily Hualapai (or Walapai) Indians. It also served some from the Apache, Havasupai, Hopi, Navajo, Pima, Tohono O'odham (Papago), and Yavapai tribes. Executive orders signed by President William McKinley created the 634.95-acre reserve in 1898.

Native American children all over were taken from their traditional homes—sometimes hundreds of miles from home—to attend boarding schools.
COURTESY GAIL L. JENNER COLLECTION

The federal government selected the location because it lies within the traditional territory of the Hualapai people. For many Hualapai students, life at the Truxton Canyon Training School—much like life at other Native American boarding schools—was often a traumatic experience. Separation from families, suppression of traditions and native languages, along with harsh discipline for infractions, was distressing and destructive. Moreover, the introduction of diseases, such as smallpox, measles, influenza, and tuberculosis, caused many students to fall ill and even die.

Another Arizona school that was created to instruct Native American students was the Phoenix Indian School, founded in 1891. Originally called the United States Industrial Indian School at Phoenix, it was a coeducational boarding school.

Native American children were brought to the school from their reservations, again, under the philosophy that they be educated and assimilated into the white man's culture. There was a large schoolhouse, several dormitories, a shop for vocational education, a dining hall, employee residential quarters, and other buildings. In addition, the school supported acres of fields where hay and produce were grown and livestock raised.

The Phoenix Indian School was a boarding school supported by the federal government.
COURTESY OF LIBRARY OF CONGRESS

It wasn't until 1988 that President Ronald Reagan signed the act by Congress to close the school and transfer its administration from the Bureau of Indian Affairs to the National Park Service. The last graduating class of nineteen students accepted their diplomas in May 1990. The grounds have since been made into Steele Indian School Park, and almost all related buildings have been demolished.

As attitudes and recognition of the issues facing Native American education evolved, federal policies reflected the change. The appointment of John Collier in 1933 as Indian commissioner helped the government move from a policy of "assimilation" to one of "self-determination." A day school was opened for the Hualapai at Peach Springs and shortly after that, the Truxton Canyon Training School closed.

CALIFORNIA

The most important event affecting the growth of the western states was the California gold rush of 1848–49. Although most people today have heard of the Mother Lode and the Sierra Nevada mining sites, few realize the scope of the gold rush. The entire northern region of California and southern region of Oregon was opened up on the heels of the forty-niners as thousands flooded San Francisco (then known as Yerba Buena) and Sacramento on the way to the gold-laden rivers and steep mountain slopes. While some miners prospered, most failed, and this propelled them deeper into the Sierra Nevada or north into the rugged Trinity, Siskiyou, and Cascade ranges.

In July 1846, two years before the first discovery of gold at Sutter's Mill, and three years before the raising of the US flag over California, the first Mormon colonists to arrive in Yerba Buena made the journey via a chartered cargo ship, the *Brooklyn*. The more

Miners headed into the northern California mountains

than two hundred exiled Mormons sought a new home; one hundred of these "Pacific Pilgrims" were children. Because there was little housing available in the city, however, a number of the Mormon families moved south. One group settled at Mission Dolores, the other at Mission Santa Clara. The two schools set up inside rather dilapidated outbuildings found at each location were the first in California to teach in English.

The group that remained in Yerba Buena established a third school. Sam Brannan, a Mormon leader, built a large home in the city, and he donated the back of his lot for the first authentic schoolhouse to be built in what is now California. Classes began in 1847. Within four years, there were 11,252 children enrolled in one-room schools up and down California. By 1854, there were almost twenty thousand children and 169 official schools.

The 1850 US California census, the first census that included all non-Indian people, showed 7,019 females, including 4,165 non-Indian females older than age fifteen.

Inducements to sail to California were posted all over the East.
COURTESY GAIL L. JENNER COLLECTION

However, to this should be added another 1,300 women (older than fifteen) living in San Francisco, Santa Clara, and Contra Costa counties where censuses were lost and not included in the recorded totals.

By 1852, the state population increased to about two hundred thousand, of which roughly 10 percent were female. According to the 1860 census, California's population totaled 330,000 individuals, with 223,000 males and 107,000 females. By 1870, the population had increased to 560,000 with 349,000 males and 211,000 females—or a ratio of 100 males to 38 females.

In San Francisco, the port of entry for California's steamships, the population exploded from two hundred in 1846 to thirty-six thousand in 1852. The immediate problem of housing led to the construction of canvas-covered tents and wooden structures made from the abandoned ships crowding the harbor.

Women Who Went West

With so few women residing in gold rush California, the marriage market was in a woman's favor. Mixed marriages between white males and Native American women became common in the region of the gold mines, most often because very few women were available. While intermarriage was considered taboo in the East, in

Mixed marriages were quite common in early California; this is the Lee Southard family on the Klamath, circa 1900.
COURTESY SISKIYOU COUNTY MUSEUM

the West it was quite common; the descendants of such marriages still represent a percentage of the region's pioneer families.

As women became a larger component of these isolated settlements in the 1850s and 1860s, a middle-class morality developed along with the towns, which helped encourage the building of schools.

Some women came west seeking a husband. This woman placed what might be considered one of the first personal ads in a California newspaper with the heading: "A HUSBAND WANTED: By a lady who can wash, cook, scour, sew, milk, spin, weave, hoe (can't plow), cut wood, make fires, feed the pigs, raise chickens, rock the cradle (gold rocker, I thank you, Sir!), saw a plank, drive nails, etc. . . . These are a few of the solid branches; now for the ornamental, 'long time ago' she went as far as syntax, read Murray's Geography and through two rules in Pike's Grammar. Could find six states on the atlas. Count read, and you can see that she can write. Can—no, could— paint roses, butterflies, ships, etc."

She also wrote that she "could dance once, ride a horse, donkey or oxen" and she ended her ad with: "Now for the terms. Her age is none of your business. She is neither handsome nor a fright, yet an old man need not apply,

Women worked as hard as their husbands.
COURTESY GAIL L. JENNER COLLECTION

nor any who have not a little more education [than] she has, and a great deal more gold, for there must be $20,000 settled on her before she will bind herself to perform all the above."

Robert Semple, a delegate from Solano County at the first Constitutional Convention of California, held in Monterey in 1849, wrote: "I regard education as a subject of particular importance here in California . . . here, above all places in the Union, we should have, and we possess the resources to have, a well regulated system of education. Education, sir, is the foundation of republican institutions; the school system suits the genius and the spirit of our form of government. . . . They must be educated; they must educate their children; they must provide means for the diffusion of knowledge and the progress of enlightened principles."

As demonstrated by Semple, the California legislature was encouraged "by all suitable means" to promote "the intellectual, scientific, moral and agricultural improvement" through education. With California's population growing quickly, schools were opened up and down the state. Even today, a number of rural schools remain primary centers for outlying areas, particularly in the northern part of the state.

Conditions were often primitive, but many schools were improved upon over time. The Igo Schoolhouse, now located on the fairgrounds in Anderson, California, was built circa 1872. It operated in Igo as a school for almost a hundred years.

Electricity came to Igo and the schoolhouse in 1941; but even though it had electricity, a wood stove heated the schoolhouse. Running water was added in the 1950s, but prior to that a trustee of the school was paid $1 a month to carry water in each day in a bucket. As with most early schools, the restrooms were located outside.

In 1910, fire in Igo destroyed a hotel, a store, a blacksmith shop, and a residence. Fortunately the wind was blowing away from the schoolhouse and the building was spared.

Igo Schoolhouse, now located at the Shasta County fairgrounds
COURTESY GAIL L. JENNER COLLECTION

The Douglas Flat School is the oldest surviving schoolhouse in Calaveras County, California. Built during the gold rush, circa 1854 or 1856, the building remains much as it did over 160 years ago. It continues to serve the community in a number of ways: as a church, a Sunday school, a kindergarten classroom, and a school office. It also functions as a meeting place for community activities. Reportedly, the building may have been moved to its present spot from a location closer to Coyote Creek.

Altaville Grammar School, in Calaveras County, California, was also one of the oldest schools in California. Founded in 1858, the red brick schoolhouse was built with money raised at a dance at a local saloon! It was the only schoolhouse in the community for over ninety years.

Susanne Twight-Alexander attended this school in Calaveras County, California. She is seated on the far left, second row, and is wearing a white sweater.
COURTESY SUSANNE TWIGHT-ALEXANDER

ALTAVILLE GRAMMAR SCHOOL

THIS BRICK BUILDING, ERECTED IN 1858 WITH FUNDS RAISED BY A DANCE IN THE BILLIARD SALOON OF THE N.R. PRINCE BUILDING (WHICH STILL STANDS), IS ONE OF THE OLDEST SCHOOLS OF CALIFORNIA. USED AS A SCHOOL UNTIL 1950, IT WAS THEN REPLACED BY THE PRESENT MARK TWAIN ELEMENTARY SCHOOL IN ALTAVILLE.

HISTORICAL LANDMARK NO. 499

MARKER PLACED BY THE CALIFORNIA STATE PARK COMMISSION IN COOPERATION WITH PRINCESS PARLOR NO. 84, NATIVE DAUGHTERS OF THE GOLDEN WEST, MAY 1, 1955.

Altaville Grammar School is listed on the National Register of Historic Places.

ONE ROOM

🔔

In Amador County, California, the first schoolhouse was built in Sutter Creek in 1857. That school burned in 1870 and the second school was constructed in 1871. The area was reasonably prosperous, allowing the community to build a solid two-story brick school with a low gabled roof and a small bell tower. Today the old Sutter Grammar Creek School is one of the few remaining two-story brick schoolhouses of such size and quality.

🔔

The old schoolhouse in Indio, California, was the second school to be built in the area and it served students from grades kindergarten through eighth. The school and the region grew rapidly as a result of the impact of the Southern Pacific Railroad.

The Indio schoolhouse was later used as a hospital during the great 1918 flu epidemic that took about 600,000 lives in the United States and 50 million around the world. During the 1930s, it was moved to serve as a separate classroom for Roosevelt School. Today the restored one-room schoolhouse is part of the Coachella Valley History Museum, which was established in 1965.

🔔

Anaheim, California, was originally settled by a group of German immigrants who moved from San Francisco to the southland. In September 1857 this community became the oldest "colonial settlement" established in the state.

In 1860, nine pupils attended a school in Anaheim, California. The first teacher was Fred William Kuelp. Like the simple adobe structure that housed the students, the schooling was basic.

Building a school was a serious priority. The people constructed an adobe building to be used as both a schoolhouse and an assembly hall. However, four years later, during the winter of 1861–62, the Santa Ana River overflowed and damaged the school. After the flood, school was held in the Water Company's building until 1869, when a new schoolhouse was built.

In 1877, the second schoolhouse was deemed inadequate for the increasing student population. Professor J. M. Guinn, who had been the principal of the Anaheim schools, authorized the district to sell bonds in order to generate enough money to fund a new school. The school was later reported to be the "handsomest building in the county outside of Los Angeles city" and remained in operation until 1920.

Historically, Guinn's strategy was significant; selling bonds to raise capital has become a very common method of funding new school projects throughout California.

In 1857, the Vernon School was opened in the town that is now known as Verona, in Sutter County, California. Classes were first held in a hotel and then in the town bowling alley. In 1863, a schoolhouse was built. That schoolhouse is still standing and is considered to be possibly one of the oldest standing schoolhouses in the state.

On April 2, 1866, the California Legislature approved "an act to create the County of Kern, to define its boundaries and to provide for its organization." In November of that year, the Board of Supervisors called for the organization of school districts in the communities of Tejon, Havilah, Kelso Valley, and Lynn's Valley, which no longer exists. A district was formed in Tehachapi later, in November 1866, and from thirteen students that first year, attendance grew to thirty-two in 1880–81.

The first school in Kern County, built in 1866, was a log structure located about two miles south of Bakersfield. It was about twenty feet square, but had no windows and only a simple earthen floor. It did have a fireplace at one end and roughly hewn log benches.

The first teacher was P. R. Hamilton who moved north from Los Angeles. However, he taught only three months; Mrs. Grace Ann Ranney was the second teacher. The third instructor was an elderly woman, Miss Lucy Jackson. Miss Jackson remained for two years.

The school was supported by subscription, each student paying $2.50 a month, but materials were few and there wasn't even a map or globe.

One event stood out during Miss Jackson's tenure that affected both students and teacher: A rattlesnake crawled in and curled up in the center of the room. When the children saw the snake, they rushed from the school. An older boy managed to kill the intruder, and though the students reluctantly returned, for weeks the smaller children sat with their feet drawn up under the benches. Miss Jackson soon retired from teaching.

A school in Dogtown, California, in 1911
COURTESY GAIL L. JENNER COLLECTION

Postcard of Wyandotte School in Butte County, California, signed by two teachers in May 1907
COURTESY GAIL L. JENNER COLLECTION

The La Grange School, in La Grange, Stanislaus County, California, was built in 1875. The one-room school, which featured the traditional bell tower, actually replaced a rough timber school that had been built circa 1855. The first teacher on record was C. C. Wright, from Iowa; he arrived in 1866. Wright also became an attorney and served as the district attorney of Stanislaus County from 1876 to 1879, then served in the state assembly in 1886. One of his most important pieces of legislation was the Wright California Irrigation Act, signed into law in 1887.

According to various sources, Bret Harte may have taught school at La Grange while on his way to the Sierra Gold Fields.

Bret Harte reportedly taught school at La Grange circa the 1850s.
COURTESY FORT JONES MUSEUM

The Dixie School in San Rafael, Marin County, California, was built in 1864. James Miller—who arrived in 1844—donated the property upon which Dixie School was built. The story goes that on their way west, while camped at Independence Rock, Wyoming, his wife gave birth to a little girl; they named her Ellen Independence Miller. The school was used until 1957; the last teacher was Josephine Codoni Leary.

The Dixie School is considered the oldest one-room school in Marin County, California.

The Dixie School was placed on the National Register of Historic Places in 1971.
COURTESY GAIL L. JENNER COLLECTION

The first, simple frame Spring Schoolhouse was built in 1890 and was located thirteen miles southwest of the town of Dorris, in northeastern California. In 1899, Mary M. McCraig was the teacher. Ten students attended school for six months. During the winter of 1924–25, Lester Huffman's father, tending to his dairy cows, spied the schoolhouse engulfed in flames. It burned to the ground in minutes.

While a new school was built, classes were held in a bunkhouse on the Briggs' ranch. In addition to a new school, two barns were built to house the children's horses. One story about that time period involved Lester Huffman's mother. As she was driving her children to school in her wagon, the horse nearly disappeared into a huge hole. A neighbor rushed to help her free the horse and wagon.

The Spring School was closed in April 1949, after which it stood abandoned.

In 1977, the school building was donated by the Butte Valley School District and brought to Yreka, California. It is now part of Siskiyou County Museum's "Outdoor Museum." According to director Lisa Gioia, "The Spring Schoolhouse remains a wonderful example of a one-room schoolhouse. Students from all over come to see how children in the nineteenth and early twentieth centuries lived."

At the beginning of the twentieth century, Locke was California's largest rural Chinatown, but it was in 1905 that the US Supreme Court required California to extend public education to the children of Chinese immigrants. In 1915, the local chapter of the Chinese Nationalist Party (Kuomintang) built the schoolhouse as a meeting place and town hall. From 1926 until 1940 the building also served as a school to teach the Chinese language to local children. In those days the school was known as the Kao Ming School.

Two Chinese girls pose for the camera. Gerhard Sisters, photographer.
COURTESY OF LIBRARY OF CONGRESS

Willow Creek School students, circa 1908, including (in no particular order) Josie DeAvilla, Ernest Betts, Jimmie Foster, Hermie Foster, Earl Ager, Alvie Quadrus, and Enzie Quadros.
COURTESY SISKIYOU COUNTY MUSEUM

Naomi Cooksey went to Laguna Elementary, located off Chileno Valley Road, in the beautiful ranch lands of western Petaluma, California. Built in 1906, Laguna School continues to function as an active schoolhouse while housing two newly renovated multi-age classrooms serving kindergarten through sixth grade.

Dress Code

Carol Pitts Maplesden attended East Fork School, from first to eighth grade, in the late 1920s. "There was no kindergarten in those days," she explained, "only about twelve to sixteen kids." She recalled Mrs. Ruth Rogers was one of her teachers, as was Miss California Harris, who taught for nine years. Carol and her siblings rode together by horseback to school.

One memory shared by Carol's sister Dorothy Pitts Butler involved bib overalls: "We hated dresses (there were seven girls and two boys in the Pitts family). By the time we got to school with our dresses jammed into our overalls . . . those skirts were a mess . . . [and] Sister Mary decided to do something about the problem. Mrs. Rogers asked us to go to the anteroom and remove our overalls when she saw us [still in our bibs] at our desks after the bell had rung. I, dutifully, but reluctantly, removed the offending garment. Mary sat stolidly. Mrs. Rogers quipped: 'Mary, please remove your overalls.' Mary replied, 'I can't. I haven't a dress on underneath!'"

Of course all the children giggled when Mrs. Rogers demanded to know why Mary had no dress under her coveralls. When Mary complained about what their dresses looked like after riding horseback with them stuffed into their overalls, Mrs. Rogers relented and allowed the girls to wear overalls rather than dresses.

According to Dorothy, "That is how Mary Pitts went on strike to change an unrealistic dress code at East Fork School!"

The first recorded mention of the Shasta County town of Kennett appeared in the *Daily Alta California* dated June 7, 1852, after gold had been found in Backbone Creek, the future location of Kennett. Kennett Schoolhouse was later flooded by the filling of Shasta Lake.
COURTESY GAIL L. JENNER COLLECTION

GloryAnn (Colt) Jenner attended Callahan School. One memory she shared was how the boys would eagerly run out at recess and across the East Fork of the Scott River then climb the rough cliffs and rocky ledges on the far side. "Nobody said much," she noted, "although that would never be permitted now."

She began school at age six and stayed to the sixth grade. She recalled that the bus driver, who was a junior in high school, drove the bus to school and home again. "That, too, would never be permitted these days!"

Sadly, by 1974, the population dwindled to two students—Robin and Shawn Hayden—making the school's closure necessary. Mrs. Kathy Moore was Callahan's last teacher and when it closed, she remarked, "This is a sad day for our little community."

School children at Callahan School, circa 1941. GloryAnn is second from the right in the back row, between the teacher's daughter on the left and MaryAnn Grossen on the right. Others in the photo (in no particular order) include EddyLou Garner, Herbie Wright, Steve Farrington, Bud Fowler, Bonnie Fowler, Paul Black, Mildred Wright, Joanne Black, Bev Hughes, Shirley Hayden, and Alberta Borba.
COURTESY GLORYANN JENNER

The last day of the Callahan School, 1974. Kathy Moore, the teacher, sits with Robin and Shawn Hayden, the school's last two students. The last two students to attend the Callahan School were related to the school's first teacher, Rosalea Barnum.
COURTESY SISKIYOU COUNTY MUSEUM

Lanora Phelps shared that two of her four kids attended the one-room school in Little Shasta, near Montague, Siskiyou County, California. Little Shasta School was established circa 1857, but the present building was constructed in 1875. It is actually one of the two oldest continuously running schools in the state of California and is still operating today; there is one teacher plus a part-time aide, one computer/lunch and after-school person, and thirteen kids.

Betty Davis Carrier started school at Little Shasta in the fall of 1937. Her first teacher was Mrs. Fern Meamber of Yreka, who taught all eight grades, with a total of fifteen students. Betty was one of three children in the first grade. She described the schoolhouse

Tablerock Schoolhouse and students, circa 1888
COURTESY SISKIYOU COUNTY MUSEUM

A Little Red Schoolhouse

Eugene French wrote in his memoir, *Reminiscences of the Past of Siskiyou County,* "In 1919, I began first grade in the little red schoolhouse in Klamathon [California]. It had survived all the various catastrophes to hit that town. . . . It stood alone on the hill, the surrounding buildings having been burned in the big fire or having fallen down in the passing years. . . . In the back of the school, there was a woodshed flanked on each end by the two 'restrooms.' On the west side of this building, a lean-to shed was built by the parents of the school children to shelter the horses we rode to school.

"Just before I began school, the Elmores moved from the Piver house to a new house built with the help of my father and located on the north side of the river, across from the French house and adjacent to the Crenshaw blacksmith shop. Since our ranch was about three miles from the school, I stayed with the Elmores and went to school from there.

"The red schoolhouse had three rooms, but only two of them were considered 'safe,' so we only used two of them. One for classes and one for a playroom in inclement weather. Most of the time we played outside, the usual kid games. We could run all over the hills surrounding the schoolhouse as long as we got back to class before the 'last' bell rang. The bell was a large bell on top of the house. No one used the excuse of not hearing it.

"After a couple of years, the Elmores moved into Hornbrook and I went back to the ranch in the hills and walked or rode horseback to school. All of the children attending school got there the same way, on horseback or on foot. When two or more of us met at the south end of the bridge across the river, we would race to school, about three quarters of a mile. I guess we were all pretty good riders as I don't recall any accidents.

"At the most, there were probably only twelve pupils in school at one time. Some years they represented all eight grades, sometimes only three or four grades. . . .

"Somewhere between 1924 and 1926 the little red schoolhouse burned to the ground. It happened at the beginning of Christmas vacation on the eve of our school Christmas play. . . . The cause of the fire was never determined as far as I know, but we had a large, potbellied stove in the classroom and I think the grate in the front of the stove was accidentally left open and coals or sparks flew out and set the fire. I have no photos of the little house but it is clear in my memory and many, many years later, I painted an oil of it as I remember it."

Shasta River School celebrates a reunion with several former students.
COURTESY SHARI FIOCK SANDAHL

this way: "When I first attended school, the building was heated with an oil heater, that at various times would explode into a cloud of oily soot. There was no running water in the building, so we would pull a bucket of water from a dug well in the front yard. There were two outhouses in each corner of the yard, one for the girls and one for the boys. A large closet in the center of the building held our coats, galoshes and lunches. We did have one extra room that was used as a playroom on rainy/snowy days, and it also doubled as a stage for Christmas programs and for graduation."

Another nearby school was Tablerock, located on the Davis ranch road; it was established in 1869 and terminated in 1932.

The Honolulu Schoolhouse and playground
COURTESY SISKIYOU COUNTY MUSEUM

Charles H. Fiock wrote in his memoir *It's Me, May I Come In?* about living on a farm in Shasta Valley and attending the local Shasta River School. Shasta Valley makes up a large section of Siskiyou County, not far from Yreka, the county seat. Eventually, Shasta River School joined the Yreka Elementary School District, along with other very small schools, including Cherry Creek, Mono, Ross, and the Honolulu School.

The Honolulu School was located east of the Shasta River schools, along State Route 96 on the Klamath River. Nothing remains today except a small sign, but the school was named in recognition of a group of Hawaiians—also known as "Kanakas"—who settled in the area during the gold rush.

Life on the river was not always easy, recalled Charles Fiock. In fact, one year, during wintertime, "a blizzard came and covered the valley white with snow. Then it got very cold and a blanket of fog made it hard to see. [My brothers and sisters] had to walk a mile to a one-room country school . . . the Shasta River School. [Our folks] had told [them] to stay together on the way to and from school. The mountains about the valley were so cold that coyotes would come down into the valley to find something to eat. The farmers kept their chickens in the chicken houses, the turkeys in the turkey sheds, and the pigs in the pigpens—so the coyotes got very hungry and mean. [Father said] they might even eat little boys and girls if [the coyotes] found them out by themselves.

"One day, on the way to school, our sister Mary ('Quite Contrary') decided to run ahead to talk to the teacher before any other children got to school, [but] when brothers Carl, Lloyd, Webster, and sister Kay got to the schoolhouse, Mary was not to be found! I was only four years old, but I remember Mother rang the telephone with a crank (it was like a box on the wall) and told the neighbors that Mary was lost in the snow and fog. . . . Everybody started looking for Mary.

"At the schoolhouse the children never stopped ringing the bell, loud and clear, so that Mary might hear it and find her way to the schoolhouse. Their arms became tired so they took turns ringing the bell . . . but they never stopped all day.

"When the sun was about to [set], everyone was afraid that the coyotes might be following Mary; what would happen when it got cold and dark and Mary stopped walking? The children rang the bell harder and harder and louder and louder. . . .

"[Suddenly] out of the fog came 'Merry Mary Quite Contrary!' Relieved, all the children [were able] to go home."

The little red Lagunita Schoolhouse, located on San Juan Grade Road facing Sugar Loaf Mountain, on the northern outskirts of Salinas, California, was built in 1897. The quaint, historic one-room schoolhouse served the area's children from first to eighth grade until 1967 when the building was condemned. Lagunita Schoolhouse was the one John Steinbeck wrote about in his novel *The Red Pony*.
COURTESY GAIL L. JENNER COLLECTION

Today the Centerville School has been incorporated into the Colman Community Memorial Museum complex. Locals have enthusiastically supported the museum and its efforts to preserve and display artifacts of the region. The old school is also used as a community center.
COURTESY TERESA DAVIS

Schools had to have a minimum of seven students. In 1914, a school was built in Seiad Valley near the Lowden ranches. When the number of students here grew, a larger school was built nearer the Arial Lowden Ranch, circa 1920. Teachers included Queen Huey, Geneive High, and Frances Collins in the first years, and Mrs. [Lena] Crabtree and Mrs. Burch during the 1930s and 1940s.

Shown here are the Seiad students of 1935: Top row: Vivian Prather, Dorothy Thomas, Paul Hawks, and Billy Stock; Middle row: Shirley Crawford, Donnie Thomas, Louella Hawks, Oliver Stock, and Gene Miller. Front row: Delberta Lighthill, Hazel Roberts (Gendron), Dorothy Flack, Kenny Lighthill, and Lee Stock.

The Weaverville Courthouse is the second oldest courthouse in California still in use today. It originally housed offices and a saloon that boasted the first piano in the county.
COURTESY GAIL L. JENNER COLLECTION

Pepperwood was one of the northernmost communities in Humboldt County, California, and was known for its farming and agricultural land. A number of dairies and creameries were established around the area. The post office was open from 1887 to 1892 and then again from 1901 to 1965. Two floods, one in 1955 and the other in 1964, wiped out the town. Pepperwood School was one of Humboldt County's early schools.
COURTESY GAIL L. JENNER COLLECTION

The Stone Lagoon School, north of Eureka, is known as "The Little Red Schoolhouse."
CAROL M. HIGHSMITH PHOTOGRAPHER/COURTESY OF THE LIBRARY OF CONGRESS

COLORADO

When Colorado became a state in 1876, the Western Slope was at first divided into seven counties. In 1885, these counties were redistricted so there were then eighteen. There had been some discovery of carbonate, lead, and silver deposits, but the discovery did not amount to much. Within a few months, the gold rush was over, but the rush to populate the state was still on.

🔔

From 1875 to 1892, Independence School of Fort Lupton, Colorado, was known as the Acorn Academy—named for the Acorn cattle brand used by the family who donated the land. In 1892, the students at the school changed its name to Independence School. In May of 1900, the one-room schoolhouse was replaced by a brick two-room school, leaving the original frame school to be used as a residence, often as housing for migrant farm workers.

In 1992, the Watada family donated the old schoolhouse to the South Platte Valley Historical Society and it was moved to a temporary location on the society's Fort Lupton Historic Park property. Then, in 1996, it was moved to its permanent location within Fort Lupton Historic Park. Grant money was received from the Colorado Historical Fund and private donations and volunteers provided the labor to restore the school to its original condition.

🔔

Indian Park School in Sedalia, Douglas County, Colorado, was built in 1884. Identified as District #7, the school was known by various names as well, including: Jarre Canon School, Mountain School, Brown's School (for Orville Brown who homesteaded the neighboring property), and finally Indian Park School.

William Smith purchased the land for the school in 1883. Located just north of Colorado Highway 67, ten miles west of Sedalia, the school was built in 1884. There were never more than twelve students attending the school. During the winter there was heavy snow, and it's been recorded that sometimes the snow was so deep, students could stand atop the boys' and girls' outhouses in order to lob snowballs at each other.

Unlike most schoolhouses, Indian Park School was never moved. In 1959, however, it was one of the last one-room schools in Douglas County to close. In 1974, the building was purchased by the Indian Park Schoolhouse Association and placed on the National Register of Historic Places.

🔔

Wallace Creek runs through both Mesa and Garfield Counties on its way to the Colorado River. Granlee Gulch School was one of the schools established in Garfield County. One of the early superintendents of the county was Mrs. Lucy DeWitt.

Granlee Gulch School, circa 1900
COURTESY GAIL L. JENNER COLLECTION

Montezuma is located in eastern Summit County, Colorado, at an elevation of 10,400 feet. In 2010, its population numbered sixty-five. The first school was built in 1880, but in 1884, a newer framed schoolhouse replaced it. The belfry, bell, and entry hall were added after 1884. In addition, the white clapboard siding was added to cover the brown board-and-batten walls. Interestingly, ladders were placed on the roof in case of fire, as required by the town's fire ordinances. Still, fire damaged the school in 1915, 1949, and 1958.

The school also featured two attached double-seater outhouses—one for girls and one for boys—at the back of the building. They were used until the school closed in 1958.

Young Bruce Bishop and his twin sister Barbara attended the Lebanon School in the 1950s, in the southwestern corner of the state, between Cortez and Dolores, Colorado. His family lived one and a half miles from the school, and the kids would either walk or ride horses.

There was a stable (called a "barn") behind the school, and at recess, the children were required to go tend their horses. The area was a ranching and farming community.

On the first day of school, Bruce remembered taking his Lone Ranger lunchbox to school. Both he and Barbara rode to school together. Because the school and community were located at an elevation of 6,500 feet, winters were cold—very cold. Bruce commented, "We kids would take our sleds and ride along the hill that run along the road. It was perfect for sledding." On the other hand, Bruce added, "We had an outhouse and in the winter, it was very cold. Thank goodness, in the second grade, we got indoor plumbing."

Bruce also shared, "I remember in first grade, there was a bell at the top of the school and a long rope that hung down. Mrs. Ruth Lyons would pull the rope and we kids would hang on it and go up and down. You could hear it for miles!"

Bruce credits Mrs. Lyons for instilling in him his love of learning, in particular math. "I would hurry through my own lessons so that I could do the upper level math problems."

As students entered the school, the boys' coatroom was on the right, the girls' coatroom was on the left. There was a stove that burned coal and, added Bruce, "Just inside the front door was a well, but we had to pump water and we were allowed to only get a drink at recess."

The school was built in 1907. Noted Bruce, "My grandfather, Wilbur Bishop, helped build the school, even though my father attended a different school. Both of them, however, are buried half a mile from the school."

Because Bruce's father worked in oil exploration, after second grade the family moved away. Bruce attended slightly bigger schools, in Wyoming, Utah, and other Colorado sites, but the family returned to the Lebanon school when he was in the sixth grade. "It was a rude awakening," noted Bruce, because by then the kids were being bussed into town to a larger school.

For those traveling west, finding a community with a school was a plus. In 1859, settlers arriving in West Denver, Colorado, were pleased to note that a school had been established. Although leaky and mud-roofed, the one-room log cabin called the Union School was opened up near the corner of Twelfth and Black. O. J. Goldrick was the schoolmaster, and thirteen children were enrolled.

In 1860, the Union School moved to a shingled one-room building. The school grew so quickly that another teacher had to be hired. Then in 1862, the first East Denver School Board was elected and School District #1 was created.

The Lebanon School is closed now and has been turned into a bed and breakfast.
COURTESY BRUCE AND VONITA BISHOP

The Colorado town of Gold Hill also dates back to the early gold mining days. In January 1859, gold was discovered in Gold Run Creek located near the center of today's town of Gold Hill. By summer 1859 the town's population numbered between three and five thousand, although most of the town was little more than a tent city. The town's prosperity lasted only a few years; by the late 1860s—as the mines played out and America was thrust into the Civil War—Gold Hill was nearly deserted.

In 1872, however, with the discovery of tellurium, which was a form of gold ore heretofore overlooked, Gold Hill went through a revival. With this influx of new inhabitants, the town experienced a building boom. Twenty dwellings, six boardinghouses, a hotel, two stores, a meat market, a blacksmith shop, two stables, two saloons and a schoolhouse were built.

The first school was a log structure that served as a schoolhouse during the week and a church on Sundays. That first year there were thirty-one students taught by Miss Hannah C. Spalding, a native of Massachusetts. The October 17, 1873 issue of the *Boulder County News* named Gold Hill's new school "one of the best schools in the County."

In 1890, however, the original school was dismantled and replaced by a larger one-room frame structure, which is still used as the room for grades three to five.

Against all odds, Gold Hill School has remained in continual operation ever since the one-room log school opened in 1873, and it narrowly survived being destroyed by a wildfire in November 1894 when the entire town was saved by a dramatic change of wind and the onset of a snowstorm.

Although its enrollment has fluctuated from one student to eighty in its 135 years of operation, Gold Hill School is the longest continually operating school in Colorado.

IDAHO

Idaho was actually one of the last of the forty-eight continental states to be settled by those of European descent. The Native American tribes residing here probably numbered ten thousand (but estimates vary) before the Lewis and Clark Expedition entered the region in 1805, and a second expedition crossed southern Idaho circa 1811 or 1812. The fur trade was responsible for much of the early exploration of the region.

The first settled town in Idaho was Franklin, established by emigrating Mormons in 1860. Mormon pioneers actually established a majority of historic communities in southeastern Idaho. Immigrants from England, Ireland, and Germany also began to arrive in the late nineteenth century. In February 1879, Washington County was officially created by an act of the ninth territorial legislature.

🔔

After the arrival of the railroad, towns in Idaho grew at a rapid pace. In 1881, the Weiser School District was formed from land that was formerly a part of the lower Mann Creek of Jeffreys District. The Mann Creek Schoolhouse was a small wood frame school.

Silver City, Idaho, was established in 1864. Located on the east side of Jordan Creek in the Owyhee Mountains of southwest Idaho, Silver City was a successful mining town. The two-story wood frame school was built in 1892 and used until 1934 after the county seat was moved to Melba and Silver City's population dwindled.

Beginning in the 1960s, artifacts and other memorabilia from the community were maintained in the second story of the schoolhouse. In 1972, the school was listed on the National Register of Historic Places, and today, the Historic Silver City Foundation, Inc., owns the schoolhouse.

The town of Mora, in Ada County, Idaho, was situated on the trail to Silver City. Settled between 1907 and 1909, the Mora Schoolhouse was built in 1910 for the sum of $2,900. The school served the community until the mid-1950s when it had to be closed because of well contamination. Ironically, the school was sold in 1966 for $2,200! Today little of Mora remains.

Orchard, Idaho, also in Ada County, was laid out in 1895. Previously known as Bisuka, the town was located near the Elmore County line. Little remains except the one-room schoolhouse, which served locals from the early 1900s until 1966.

Dr. Harlan Page Ustick, a doctor and astute businessman, founded Ustick, Idaho, in 1907, when a streetcar company built a line through the area, connecting it with Boise and surrounding towns. Ustick was a highly productive agricultural area known for its vast apple orchards, and supported a school, a bank, a store, a church, a creamery, and vinegar processing plants. It was written that Ustick had "the finest orchard in the Boise Valley."

The Ustick School, a four-room building, was constructed between 1909 and 1911. It was a cream-colored two-story brick building with a cedar-shingled roof. Built in the colonial revival style, the front porch boasted Ionic columns and a round arch framed the door. Windows were seven feet tall. The interior of the school was paneled and the detailed woodwork reflected Craftsman-style touches.

The Bellgrove School, in Kootenai County, Idaho, was built in 1918, after the land—which had been within the boundary of the Coeur d'Alene Reservation—was relinquished to the US government by treaty. An earlier school had preceded the 1918 schoolhouse; in addition, two log schoolhouses in a nearby area also preceded it. Heavy logging and a fire in 1910 adversely affected the region. Bellgrove School was used until 1958, when it was brought into the Worley School District.

A number of wood frame one-room schools were built in Kootenai County, Idaho, circa the turn of the twentieth century.
COURTESY GAIL L. JENNER COLLECTION

Meridian, Idaho, is located on the Snake River basin plain at the south end of the state. The community's earliest settlers lived along Five Mile Creek, where water runs year-round. Eliza Ann Zenger filed Meridian's town site on homestead grant land in 1893; she and her husband had come from Utah.

Around 1900, the area's farmers established fruit orchards, in particular apples and prunes, and built fruit packing businesses and prune dryers alongside the railroad tracks. The town's one-room school began classes in 1904; the school was located at the corners of Pine Street and Meridian Road.

School children and teacher having a picnic outside their Idaho schoolhouse
COURTESY GAIL L. JENNER COLLECTION

KANSAS

In 1854, passage of the Kansas–Nebraska Act opened Kansas and Nebraska to settlement. The rush was on to find good land. Settlers poured in from Iowa, Missouri, Ohio, Illinois, Kentucky, and many other states. The early days of Kansas settlement was a race between Free Staters and Slaveholders that would determine how Kansas would be admitted to the Union. Conflicting constitutions were passed and Kansas engaged in a number of bloody conflicts even before the Civil War.

A second rush into Kansas took place after the Civil War and the passage of the Homestead Act—which offered 160 acres of land to anyone who could "prove" a claim. For a hundred years, white frame or native stone one-room schoolhouses were spread across the section corners of Kansas, with names like Prairie Flower, Buzzard Roost, and Good Intent. Children across the state often had to endure harsh weather, dust storms, and prairie fires on the way to or from school.

The schoolteacher, sometimes only a little older than her pupils, was a renaissance individual. She had to be a nurse, janitor, musician, philosopher, peacemaker, wrangler, fire stoker, baseball player, professor, and poet—all for less than $50 a month. From the early 1800s to about 1950, at least nine thousand one-room schools operated throughout Kansas. By 1945, the number of schools dropped to 7,200.

The materials used in constructing Kansas schools depended on the area's physical landscape. In eastern Kansas, schools like Arvonia were built of native limestone, or, as with the Shawnee Indian Mission, of brick. Many schools throughout Kansas were built of wooden clapboard, such as the German Lutheran School. In western Kansas, some early schools, like the Thomas County School, were made from sod because of the lack of timber or stone. Often called "Nebraska marble," most soddies were characterized by a dirt floor and a mud roof and few if any windows. The soddies often attracted rats, rodents, and other "varmints." On the other hand, because of the heavy walls, which were often three feet thick, soddies were often cool in the summer and warm in the winter.

The District #34 school in Chase County, Kansas, was built of native limestone in 1896. Even the two outhouses were built of limestone. The Lower Fox Creek School in Strong City, Kansas, built on land donated by Steven F. Jones, was also built of native limestone. Built in 1882, it remained in operation until 1930. Today it is part of the Tallgrass Prairie National Preserve.

The distinction of the first school in Kansas goes to the Shawnee Indian Mission School, a brick school constructed in 1839. Reverend Thomas Johnson, for whom Johnson County is named, founded the school. The mission, which he established in 1832, was located outside Kansas City. At its height, the mission encompassed two thousand acres with sixteen buildings, including three brick buildings that housed male and female students and teachers. The school had an enrollment of nearly two hundred Indian boys and girls from the ages of five to twenty-three. Today the boys' building is a museum.

Columbus, Kansas, is situated in Cherokee County, in the southeastern corner of the state. The town was named for Columbus, Ohio, and the first settlement occurred around 1868. The post office was established the next year. The importance of Columbus was that it served as a junction for the Saint Louis–San Francisco and the Missouri–Kansas–Texas Railways.

The Golden Rule School #68 in Columbus, Kansas, circa 1890–1910
COURTESY GAIL L. JENNER COLLECTION

🔔

Maxine Averill recalled that she taught at Kaw Valley from 1934 to 1935 for $57.50 a month, which was higher than the average $35 to $40 monthly salary. The school had kerosene lights and a large coal stove in the back of the room. Students had their own drinking cups and had to draw well water. Outside toilets were northwest of the building.

The school closed from 1946 to 1948, and then the district voted 19–6 in 1948 to permanently close the school. Leonard Hadl bought the schoolhouse at auction and dismantled it. Pearson Davis bought the site, and Kenneth Tuggle built a home on the site in 1952.

🔔

The town of Lanesfield was established in 1859 and served as a mailstop along the Santa Fe Trail. The school was built in 1869, but when the railroad bypassed Lanesfield—also in 1869—the town of Edgerton took root. Many of the buildings were moved to Edgerton from Lanesfield, with the exception of the one-room school. In 1903, Lanesfield School was struck by lightning and the interior of the school had to be rebuilt.

Miss Minnie Kissick's Sunday school class in Mt. Hope, Kansas, reflects how single young teachers were expected to support all levels of social interaction.
COURTESY GAIL L. JENNER COLLECTION

Homecoming

One of the most fascinating schools to be built on the high plains of Kansas was in the small settlement of Nicodemus, established at the end of Reconstruction after the Civil War. Over three hundred former slaves from Kentucky arrived by train at Ellis, Kansas. From Ellis, the refugees walked for two days before reaching their destination—the all black town known as Nicodemus.

Although the landscape was harsh, with little to recommend it, those who settled here were determined to make it their home. They built crude dugouts, but winter came quickly and the settlers were ill prepared. As the people struggled to survive, a small band of Osage Indians arrived, just in time to share the game they'd secured on a recent hunt.

The town council of Boley, Oklahoma, which was another prairie town settled by African-Americans

COURTESY GAIL L. JENNER COLLECTION

In the spring, a second group of former slaves arrived to settle in Nicodemus, but disheartened by the sparse landscape and its few resources, many returned to Kentucky while some moved on to other locations. The next year, in 1879, the last large group of former slaves arrived. During the 1880s Nicodemus flourished and grew to a town of almost seven hundred. Sadly, however, when the railroad failed to pass through the town, many residents simply left.

The District No. 1 school was built in 1917 and remained open until 1955. Education was intensely important to the people of Nicodemus, as stated by one resident (quoted in *Exodusters: Black Migration to Kansas After Reconstruction* by Nell Irvin Painter): "I wants my children to be educated then I can believe what they tells me. If I go to another person with a letter in my hand, and he reads it, he can tell me what he pleases in that letter, and I don't know any better."

While the town struggled to survive, the town of Nicodemus has continued to attract visitors, and those who return "home" to Nicodemus still celebrate the town's creation after Emancipation. Today, the annual celebration is more aptly referred to as the "Homecoming."

In 1976, Nicodemus was designated a National Historic Landmark District and became the oldest and only remaining all black town west of the Mississippi River. In 1996, the Nicodemus National Historic Site came under the management of the National Park Service.

Many of the school's teachers boarded with the Dillie family. As single young women, they were expected to contribute to the community in addition to teaching the area's children.

🔔

The South Bloomfield School in Goessel, Kansas, was built by a group of Mennonite immigrants who left their village of Alexanderwohl in Russia to settle in America where they could practice their faith. Attracted to the area by the Atchison, Topeka and Santa Fe Railway, these settlers valued education. While the first schools were held in homes, eventually enough one-room schools were built so that the distance between each school was only (or no more than) two miles. These structures were of a different construction than the more traditional rectangular-shaped schools seen in other parts of the country. Instead, they were shaped in an I-form, with a small entry, clapboard siding, and three windows on either side. The South Bloomfield School was built in this style in 1874. Charles Munger was the school's first schoolmaster and was paid $33.50 for a three-month school term.

Emma Morris began teaching in Kansas when she was eighteen years old.
COURTESY BILL SCOTT

In 1892, a new school was built to replace the original South Bloomfield School; this school was used until the 1950s. Today it sits on the grounds of the Mennonite Heritage Museum.

Bill Scott (an author who writes as "James Scott") wrote, "My grandmother, Emma Morris—who was born in 1869—taught in a one-room school from about 1885 to 1894. A fresh graduate of the Ladies' Seminary in Minneapolis, this [teaching assignment] was her first job."

Bill wrote, "It was in Lenexa, Kansas, a town so small it may no longer exist. Teaching at a one-room multi-grade school with a passel of farm kids must have been daunting to a teenager on her first assignment, but she made a go of it."

Bill added, "In 1894, she met and married my grandfather, and they moved to Chicago where he was a successful grain broker. I still have her old classroom record book, which is now about 135 years old. It contains lists of students in her classes, assignments, and grades for such things as 'deportment', an old word for classroom behavior. She was also a writer, and I have a couple of stories she wrote, and some poetry. Maybe I get my writing talent from her."

This is one of Emma's poems, which she wrote in her twenties:

I'm glad I have a good-sized slate,
With lots of room to calculate.
Bring on your sums! I'm ready now;
My slate is clean and I know how.
But don't you ask me to subtract,
I like to have my slate well packed;
And only two long rows, you know;
Make such a miserable show;
And please, don't bring me sums to add;
Well, multiplying's just as bad;
And say! I'd rather not divide
Bring me something I haven't tried!

The schoolhouse where Emma Morris first taught, in Lenexa, Kansas
COURTESY BILL SCOTT

MONTANA

As in California, the discovery of gold in Montana in 1862 and 1863 attracted people from all over. In response to the rapid growth, the Territory of Montana was created in May 1864 by an act of Congress. The territory was larger in size than all six New England states, plus New York, New Jersey, Delaware, and Maryland.

Along with gold, the Homestead Act helped to open up Montana. In fact, Montana became the most important homestead state; more than 250,000 emigrants rushed to stake their claims on thirty-two million acres.

By 1910, waves of homesteaders crossed into Montana where they began to plow up the land that had been the homeland of various tribes for generations. The windswept plains of Montana were not easy to cultivate or tame, and many of the homesteaders left in despair. Those who stayed, however, were the most rugged and determined, and building schools was as much a part of their dream as establishing homes and communities.

Homesteaders, circa 1915, breaking the sod
COURTESY GAIL L. JENNER COLLECTION

As noted in the 1881 Montana school census, out of the 9,479 children listed across the state, 5,000 attended 132 public schools. And in 1899, the first course of study for all public schools was adopted by the legislature. By 1920, the number of one-room schools in Montana totaled over 2,600.

The names of some of these historic one-room schools located across Montana's fifty-six counties reflect either the historic names of the area's settlers or some aspect of its surrounding physical landscape, such as Tom Miner, Iron Rod, Wisdom, Divide, Salmon Prairie, Yaak, Wolf Creek, Sunset, Target Range Little White, New Chicago, Sleeping Child, Fishtrap, Pig Eye, Box Elder, Second Creek Shool, Lennep, Big Elk, Howie, Dry Fork, Pontricina, Hay Coulee, SY, Seventy-Nine, Belltower, Rattlesnake, South Stacey, Flatwillow, Cutting, Navajo, Duck, Wide Awake, and Snake Creek.

One amusing anecdote involved the Old Star School in Cutbank, Montana. According to an account collected by Andrew Gulliford in his book, *America's Country Schools,*

A fellow came riding into Cut Bank, Montana, one day and stopped at the livery stable to rest his horse. He asked the blacksmith if he knew where any of the Kipp family members lived in the area. The Kipp family was one of the first white settlers in the area and there were lots of them. "Well, you know it's too bad about them Kipps," the blacksmith said. "Oh, what happened?" "Well, they had a big family reunion at the Old Star School. It was the only building big enough to hold 'em all. Well, they got to dancin', drinkin', and cavortin' around so much, that someone hit the stove and the stove pipe fell down on 'em all and killed all but a hundred of 'em."

In 1976, the dilapidated Grant Creek School, built circa 1907, was relocated to Fort Missoula. The school had closed in 1940 and was bought and used as a storeroom. Assisted by volunteers, including a chapter of Delta Kappa Gamma sorority, the school was moved to Fort Missoula and carefully restored.

It is assumed that the first school in Montana was held at Fort Owen in 1861, most specifically for the children of the men at the fort. But there is some discrepancy over whether there was a school in Bannock, Montana (the first territorial capital), as early as 1862 and 1863. According to Mrs. Frank E. Curtis, who arrived in Bannock in September 1862, "There were very few children in camp in the first winter and no school at all." Mrs. Henry Zoller did open a private school during the summer of 1863.

The city of Twin Bridges boasts Montana's oldest standing one-room school. It opened in 1867 and closed in 1873.

The first school district organized in Montana was at Virginia City. In 1864, the schoolhouse—which was actually built to be a church—measured fifty feet long by thirty feet wide. Eighty-one pupils registered for school, but no textbooks were to be had—except for whatever families could provide. School opened on March 5, 1866, and ended in mid-August. Before school resumed, an actual log schoolhouse was built.

In 1865, the first school in Bozeman, Gallatin County, was held in the back room of a log store. Miss Florence Royce taught in the second school, in the winter of 1866–67. In 1868, Miss Royce transferred to the first school to be built in Gallatin City, which was also the first school to be constructed with public funds and was built in 1868 and 1869. It cost $500.

In 1874, the Masons built a school in Bannack, Beaverhead County, Montana. It served as both a school and a hall for the Masonic Lodge. The school was unusual in that it was a grand two-story structure with a classical Tuscan design. Most schools by the 1880s and 1890s followed a similar construction, whether made of stone, rock, adobe, or plank. And most schools in Montana were one story, so such a grand structure must have provided

Bannack Schoolhouse was built by Masons in 1874.
COURTESY GAIL L. JENNER COLLECTION

Sand Springs School

Sand Springs, in Garfield County, was settled at the turn of the twentieth century by sheep, cattle, and horse ranchers. Named for the sandy soil of its landscape, as well as the number of springs found there, the town's main industry has remained agriculture. Much of the land is only suitable for grazing due to the terrain and elevation.

Sand Springs School is a one-room schoolhouse that serves kindergarten through eighth grade. Heidi Thomas, an author of western fiction and nonfiction, recalled her childhood spent at the school. She wrote, "When I was approaching school age, there were no school age kids in the area and no school closer than twenty or thirty miles away. I was so eager to learn to read and write that my parents consulted the county superintendent of schools who recommended teaching me to read from the *Mac and Muff* pre-primer series. I was in seventh heaven. Now I could read and write my own books!

"By that next summer, the Joe Dutton family moved to Sand Springs and bought the general store. They had four children, three of school age, so the neighbors got together, formed a school board, and hired a teacher, Miss Susie Huston from the Brusett, Montana area.

"There had been a school at Sand Springs, so the parents pitched in to clean and fix up the old building, which was in the middle of a field a quarter mile from the store. A coatroom was converted into a 'teacherage'—living quarters for the teacher with a bed, dresser, and a stove. With no indoor plumbing, it sported two outhouses behind the school.

"I started school with one boy and me in the first grade, one in the third, and a girl in the fourth. For several years, we were the only students. The largest school population was during my brother's time in the early '60s, with twelve students."

"I have fond memories of 'Huston,' as [our teacher] preferred to be called, teaching us in innovative ways—board games for math, 'Go-Fish' type card games for vocabulary words, and pictures she cut out from magazines as writing prompts.

"Listening to the upper grade students also piqued my interest and spurred my quest for learning. When I reached the upper grades, I helped the younger kids with their studies. Huston taught there for three years before she retired."

"Apparently the school population has come full circle," according to Sandy Gibson, postmistress and owner of the Sand Springs Store, with four students. "They now have a male teacher and attend four days a week. Innovative teaching is still the 'norm' with lots of 'hands-on' projects, such as planting and caring for trees, even a bow-and-arrow class."

Gateway to Yellowstone

Located a few miles north of Gardiner on the west bank of the Yellowstone River, Cinnabar was once considered the gateway to Yellowstone National Park. The remains of the once-thriving community of Cinnabar became a part of the park in 1932.

Hugo Hoppe, a successful freighter, founded Cinnabar in 1883—even as the Northern Pacific Railroad established the town as the last stop on its line from Livingston to the border of Yellowstone National Park. From Cinnabar, tourists would take stagecoaches to the park's north entrance. However, in 1902, the park's boundaries were extended, so the railroad moved its depot further on down the line, and the town was abandoned. The Cinnabar post office closed in 1903.

Established in 1872, Yellowstone was the United States' first national park. Various Native American tribes have lived and traveled the Yellowstone region for more than eleven thousand years, as authenticated by oral histories and archaeological research. It is known that Kiowa, Blackfeet, Cayuse, Coeur d'Alene, Bannock, Nez Perce, Shoshone, and Umatilla, among others, used the resources of the area. European Americans did not begin exploring the region until the 1800s, and the first organized expedition explored Yellowstone in 1870.

Today nothing remains of Cinnabar except some depressions in the landscape where buildings once stood. Recent archaeological digs and research will help determine if the site might be included on the National Register of Historic Places.

an imposing sight. Stairs were attached along the east wall and served as the entrance to the Masonic Hall.

🔔

The Cinnabar Basin School near Gardiner, Park County, Montana, was built in 1916 on land owned by Joseph Stermitz Sr. Many of the settlers here were looking to work in the coal mines.

In 2009–2010, the Stermitz family renovated the schoolhouse. Not only did the family work to preserve the structure and maintain its historic integrity, it is now rented out as a place to stay. Many original artifacts are on display inside the old schoolhouse.

🔔

Joe Wheeling's family lived right on the Montana/North Dakota border, where Joe attended the one-room Squaw Gap School. Both of Joe's parents had attended one-room

Squaw Gap School nearly straddles the Montana/North Dakota border.
COURTESY JOE AND JENNIFER WHEELING

schools, and his paternal grandfather also taught at one—in addition to being a rancher. Interestingly, Joe's family's mailing address was in Sidney, Montana, but the phone number (when it was finally brought in) was provided by a North Dakota company. This region was one of the last to get telephone service.

According to Joe, "For a while, we had to use the reservation phone, and we would get calls from all over. Whoever was nearby would answer the phone."

From first to eighth grade, there was only one other student in Joe's class, and he was the only boy for two to three years. There were seven students in the school when he enrolled in first grade, but enrollment dropped, and most of the time there were only four to five pupils.

Joe remembers that teachers who were exceptionally good encouraged him to move on. "They would push you and then let you go. By Christmas, I might be done with, say, one of the math books, so they would let me start on the next. It was a wonderfully 'fluid' approach to lesson planning."

He added, "For everyone there was a great sense of community. We kids took turns putting the flag up or down each day. And I cannot remember a time we didn't take a recess outside—in spite of the harsh winter conditions."

The playground was a favorite place; even the first graders played "keep away" football, although one time a bigger boy "popped me on the back and broke my collar bone." In winter, Joe said, "We rode toboggans and sleds down the hill near the school. Sometimes we would be having so much fun, the teacher would have to come out to get us, and then we were tardy (which brought on a consequence)."

Most of the land surrounding the school was either ranchland or US Forest Service land. There was no bus to ride to school, so Joe walked three miles via the main road. The high school was located about thirty-five miles away—meaning that sometimes in bad weather, students stayed with friends or neighbors rather than risking the drive home.

After high school graduation, Joe attended Colorado State University where he majored in pre-vet/animal science, then attended the Wharton School of Business

Celebrating the construction of a new schoolhouse in Melstone, Montana, circa 1900
COURTESY GAIL L. JENNER COLLECTION

where he obtained his MBA. Joe and his wife Jennifer now ranch on her family's ranch in Colorado.

As of this writing, Montana still has seventy single-teacher schools, down from 112 in 1990. However, today there are still more operating one-room schools in Montana than in any other state in the nation.

NEBRASKA

When the Mexican War began in 1846, there was no Nebraska, only a vast plain called "the Nebraska country." In fact, it was a part of a still greater territory that had been set apart by Congress in 1834. The land was deemed "Indian country," from which white settlers were excluded; however, as emigrants moved west, the territory quickly became known to them.

According to *Pioneer Stories of Cass County, Nebraska*, published by the Cass County Historical Society, "In the early fifties [1850s] a startling headline appeared in the eastern papers, 'Gold Discovered in Nebraska.' In truth, this was not an error because at that time the Territory of Nebraska included much of Colorado, all of Wyoming, Montana and the two Dakotas."

Emigrants set up tent cities as they scrambled to stake out their claims.
COURTESY GAIL L. JENNER COLLECTION

Thus, on June 24, 1854, by proclamation of President Pierce, the Territory of Nebraska was thrown open for settlement and emigrants hurriedly crossed the Missouri to stake out their claims.

Miss Adelaide Goodwill ran the first school in Omaha, in 1855. The first school in Lancaster County was established in 1865, in the dugout home of John Cadman. Small, but not quaint, the walls, ceiling, and roof were made with sod, mud, and straw.

Schools of this character, using local materials and perhaps appearing more rustic, are termed "vernacular," or "folk vernacular." All across the plains, schools appeared in a variety of temporary or vernacular construction. The first school in Alliance, Nebraska, was actually a tent. Tents were also used frequently in Nevada, Utah, and Wyoming.

Unfortunately, though sod or mud structures were sturdy and relatively insulated against cold and heat, they were susceptible to rain, especially since they characteristically had dirt floors. They were also susceptible to infestation by rodents and snakes. A sod school in Logan County, Nebraska, built circa 1890, was barely large enough to hold three students, yet the school was also the teacher's residence, with only a bed and some cooking paraphernalia provided.

One sod school in Thomas County, Nebraska, was a dugout school but also boasted a clapboard front façade. Another school in Scotts Bluff County, Nebraska, was built of baled straw walls, with a sod roof and dirt floor. It was barely seven feet high. Reportedly, grazing cattle "devoured" the school in two years. Another Nebraska school in Custer County was also built into a hillside, but along its sides the cornstalks used to keep the stove burning were often rifled through by hogs.

While sod structures were used frequently, when money was available, residents built frame schools, although even as late as 1934, a sod high school was built in the Sandhills of Nebraska so that students could pursue a secondary education closer to home. A teacherage was also built of sod, as were the privies and a barn. To heat the school, students and teacher collected cow patties, which burned easily.

🔔

The Red-Brick School House, in Blakely Township, Nebraska, was open from 1872 to 1967. By the time it closed, it was the oldest continuously used one-room school in the township. It served not only as a school, but also as a church, meeting hall, polling place, and social and political center of the community. Blakely Township is one of twenty-four townships in Gage County and over 80 percent of the population is of German descent.

In the middle of the Nebraska prairie, just west of the Homestead National Monument of America's visitor center, stands a small red brick schoolhouse. Built in 1872, it replaced an earlier log structure. The school is known as the Freeman School; however, there is disagreement on how it got its name. According to one report, "It is unclear if the school was named for homesteader Daniel Freeman, or for the brick maker, Thomas Freeman."

While Daniel Freeman was the first homesteader in Blakely Township, the new school building was made of red-orange bricks that came from the kiln of Thomas Freeman, and both served on the local school board. The school was well reputed, with schoolbooks provided to the children in 1881, "a decade before the state of Nebraska required schools to do so."

The Freeman School operated from 1872 to 1967, and when it closed, it was considered one of the oldest operating schools in Nebraska. The National Park Service decided to preserve the school because of its important role in the pioneer history of the state. In 1973, the National Park Service initiated work to return the school to its pre-1900 appearance. It is now an historic landmark and attracts visitors from all around the state.

In 1869, Hanover, Nebraska's first school building was built at the north edge of town. It was a one-story stone building. In 1879, a second building was constructed, large enough to accommodate the increased student enrollment.

An old school side by side with the new school, being built. Note the ladder and the outhouses.
COURTESY GAIL L. JENNER COLLECTION

The Children's Blizzard

Of course, on the plains weather was of paramount importance, especially for those on farmsteads or for children who attended school any distance away. One tragic event reveals the impact of weather on a community.

This story was retold in Josey Brady's *Education in the 1800s*, about life in Nebraska: "It was January 12th, 1888—The very day a powerful blizzard swept across Nebraska. With a whopping 30 to 40 degrees below 0, it is said that the temperature fell about 100 degrees in only 24 hours as the storm came with no warning! Surprisingly, there wasn't a great amount of snow but blinding wind speeds created white outs, tearing frozen eyelids open.

"This fierce storm lasted 12 to 18 hours straight, as 230 perished at their very doors. It has been ranked as Nebraska's most severe storm. If you go to visit Nebraska's capital, you'll see a mosaic on the wall of this terrifying storm from over 120 years ago. This blizzard is sometimes referred to as 'The Schoolchildren's Blizzard.' It affected children of the area greatly as well as parents, teachers, and one brave woman named Minnie Freeman who lived in Ord, Nebraska.

"She led her students through the storm with twine to a shelter after the blistering wind tore the roof off the schoolhouse. It's been said that Freeman saved nearly 16 lives that day, which was quite a lot considering most died right at their doorstep as soon as they took a step out into the below 0 temperature and ear nipping winds.

"Most of the children were kept in the schoolhouse for a full 2 days (including their youngest student who was 5 years old), waiting for rescuers to arrive as their arms grew limp and sore from ringing bells day and night to let the rescuers know where they were and that they were okay.

"Lois May Roce unfortunately didn't have the luck Minnie Freeman had. She lost most of her students before they even stepped outside the classroom. Her stove was no match for the blistering cold. She tried to take her remaining three students at the ages of 9, 9, and 6, to a farmhouse 200 yards away, but they lost each other and the children perished, leaving the teacher crawling blindly through the dangerous storm because of her horribly frost bitten feet. She made it to the farmhouse, panting, her feet fully frost bitten, and numb. She later had to have them amputated."

Such events seem incomprehensible to us, but tragedy was not an uncommon occurrence for those early settlers who were determined to carve out a home in spite of overwhelming odds.

Scenes and Incidents from the Recent Terrible Blizzard in Dakota on January 12, 1888. The storm came with no warning, and some accounts say that the temperature fell nearly 100 degrees in just 24 hours. The blizzard killed 235 people including many children. *Frank Leslie's Weekly*, January 28, 1888.

G. H. Hollenberg, founder of Hanover, was quoted as saying, "Our educational advantages are almost as good as can be found anywhere in the state. A fine stone school-house graces one of the beautiful eminences of the town, situated on one of the more prominent natural rises which characterize the town."

🔔

Harmony School, or School District #53, was a one-room schoolhouse located in Otoe County, Nebraska. The building was built in 1879 and used until 1997. In the 1930s, there were forty-two students crammed into the school building. Harmony School was the longest operating one-room schoolhouse in Nebraska, serving its community for 118 years. Today the school is privately owned.

🔔

Miss Grace Hurlbut, Bev Scott's maternal grandmother, obtained her teaching certificates and then received a teaching contract for Hooker County, Nebraska, beginning in 1897. She stopped teaching when she married O. H. Moody.

O. H. Moody, Bev's grandfather, also obtained teaching certificates and then received a teaching contract from Custer County, Nebraska, beginning in 1895. Later on he also served as a school superintendent, until he returned home to take over the family farm.

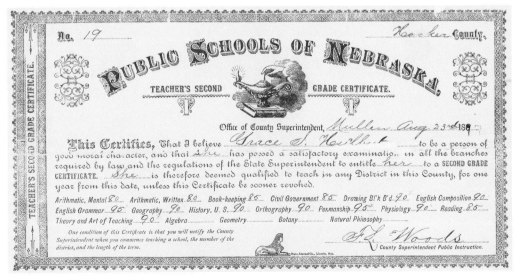

Grace Hurlbut obtained her second grade teaching certificate in 1897.
COURTESY BEV SCOTT

O. H. Moody obtained his first grade teaching certificate on August 17, 1895.
COURTESY BEV SCOTT

Bev's paternal grandmother, Eva Ellen Russell Scott, actually became the first school superintendent in Thomas County, Nebraska. She also stepped in to teach at May School when her nephew, Lloyd Krickbaum, went off to war in 1917.

🔔

Interestingly, many women served as school or county superintendents. The first woman in the country to hold the position of state superintendent was Laura Eisenhuth, in 1893, of North Dakota. But women were voting in school elections by 1890 in fifteen states and territories. In Republic County, Kansas, women served frequently as county superintendents. The first was Lucy Howard, in 1896. In Albany County, Wyoming, women served from 1885 to 1937, and in Brown County, Nebraska, only one man was elected to the position during a seventy-eight-year period, from 1897 to 1975.

Students stand in front of May School, Thomas County, Nebraska, circa 1917.
COURTESY BEV SCOTT

In Omaha, Nebraska, far more women than men served as teachers.
COURTESY GAIL L. JENNER COLLECTION

In 1984, of the 835 one-room schools still operating around the country, Nebraska had the highest number of one-room schools, with 360, but that number has dwindled considerably. In remote rural counties such as Sioux County, the schools were an important addition to the social and economic fabric.

NEVADA

Mining began at Goodsprings Township in southern Clark County, Nevada, as early as 1856 when emigrating Mormons from Las Vegas opened a lead mine at Potosi. The Goodsprings or Yellow Pine Mining District was established in 1882 and named for Joseph Good, whose cattle watered at a spring in the southeastern foothills of the Spring Mountains. Goodsprings became one of the most productive mining districts in Clark County; lead, silver, copper, zinc, and gold were all mined there.

The first Goodsprings School was established in 1907—in a tent—and Miss Winifred Hardy served as its first teacher. A schoolhouse was erected in 1913, and it is the oldest school in Clark County to be built as a school and continues to be used today. Its centennial was celebrated in 2013.

Washoe City, eighteen miles south of Reno, was established in 1860 as a lumbering camp for Virginia City. The foothills near Washoe Lake were covered with trees and there was an unlimited supply of waterpower, which could be used to power the lumber mills. Settled circa 1861, Washoe City became an important center for the surrounding farms, sawmills, and quartz mills. Ore wagons made their way daily to Virginia City.

Members of the International Order of Odd Fellows (IOOF) and Masons built the school; the lodges also helped build a hospital and several churches. Though the population soared to nearly six thousand by the mid-1860s, eventually the mining and milling economies declined, and the Washoe City post office closed in 1894. Today Washoe City is a ghost town.

Dayton, Nevada, is one of the state's most historic towns. It is located twelve miles northeast of Carson City, in Lyon County. Gold was discovered in nearby Gold Canyon in 1849. A tent trading post was established, which served westward emigrants as they passed through the area.

The first permanent building was built in the early 1850s and by 1857–58 there was a small town. At first the town was known as Chinatown because of the influx and number of Chinese miners working the local streams. As with so many mining communities, in 1859, many settlers began moving north, to the center of the Comstock mining activity, leaving only a few families behind.

Then, in 1861, Chinatown was renamed Dayton. It saw a resurgence of activity as it became a busy commercial and transportation hub. By 1865, its population

Miners flocked to Nevada as new mine sites were located. FAWCETT WALDON, PHOTOGRAPHER. COURTESY LIBRARY OF CONGRESS

Entrance to the Comstock Mines, Dayton, Lyon County, Nevada
COURTESY LIBRARY OF CONGRESS

topped 2,500 and Dayton became the county seat. The first school was also con-structed in 1865, and the stone schoolhouse became one of the finest in the state. The floor was matted, which helped to keep the dust down, and flowers and vines were planted and placed in the windows.

Sadly, the town's luck ran out for a second time. Around 1878, as the Comstock mines played out, Dayton's fortunes declined, too. In 1909, fire destroyed the town's courthouse, and in 1911 the county seat was moved to Yerington.

🔔

The Golconda School, built in 1888, is located at Morrison and Fourth Streets in Golconda, Nevada. It remains an unusually well preserved nineteenth-century wood-frame school.

The Buena Vista One-Room Schoolhouse, in Unionville, Nevada, was built in 1871 for only $2,500. It continued to operate until 1955 and is now privately owned.

The Old Schoolhouse at Sherman Station, in Elko, Nevada, is part of the Sherman Station Visitor's Center. The school has been restored to what it most likely looked like one hundred years ago, with such features as a teacher's desk, a potbelly stove, a map, and a blackboard.

Glendale, Nevada, located one mile southeast of Sparks, is home to the oldest one-room school in Nevada. Built in 1864, it was used continuously until 1958. It was the first school to be built in the Truckee Meadows area. It started out in 1857 as a way station and trading post for westbound wagon trains, many of which crossed the Truckee River at this point. Two men—Stone and Gates—operated a toll bridge and ferry, beginning in 1860. Glendale also served as the terminus for a turnpike running almost to Virginia City.

When the Glendale school opened in 1864, it served families in Truckee Meadows. The community boasted two stores, a hotel, a mercantile, a blacksmith, and several saloons. After Reno was established in 1868, however, much of Glendale's commercial business moved away. In 1976, the school building was relocated to Reno. In 1993, it was relocated again to its current location in Sparks.

The Galena Creek Schoolhouse in Storey County, Nevada, located south of Galena Creek, was built during the heyday of Galena, sometime in the 1860s. Listed on the National Register of Historic Places in 2011, what is unusual about this schoolhouse is that it was built with hand-cut local stone.

Another unique school was the Barclay School built in Clover Valley, Nevada, circa 1905. The board-and-batten schoolhouse sported a hand-hammered copper bell tower.

An amusing account of a schoolhouse occurred in the town of Currie, Nevada. The schoolhouse had been built on a local widow's land, and she was determined to take it over, declaring "she was going to make it into a washhouse." The townspeople fought to keep it, so when the widow left by train to go to Elko for the sheriff, several teams of draft horses appeared "as if by magic." The schoolhouse, the pupils, and the teacher moved it down the road to a bit of railroad property.

As related in Andrew Gulliford's *America's Country Schools*, "When the sheriff stepped from the train that afternoon, the school was in session as usual, and he could find no sign of its ever having been on the lot in town. Strange, too, the sheriff couldn't find a single person who had seen the school on that spot."

The Elgin School in Elgin, Nevada, offered its teacher an attached teacherage—a rare treat for many early teachers. It was attached via a hallway that separated the living quarters from the classroom.

New Mexico

In 1880, New Mexico had no publicly funded school system, nor did it have a private school system, thus New Mexico's historic schoolhouses have a much more recent origin. The landscape is one of dramatic images, as seen by the image of Shiprock, located in the Navajo reservation in San Juan County. Its peak elevation is 7,177 feet. The rock is sacred, and, according to legend, it is all that remains of the giant bird that carried the Navajo to New Mexico. According to Erik Painter, a Native American historian,

> *The current Navajo Nation is on a portion of traditional lands, which are between the four sacred mountains. It is in the modern states of New Mexico, Arizona, and Utah and is 27,000 square miles, about the size of Holland and Belgium combined. There are over 300,000 enrolled members, most of whom live on or near the Navajo Nation. About 60% speak the language.*

Shiprock rises 1,583 feet above the floor of the high-desert plain.
COURTESY GAIL L. JENNER COLLECTION

Raton, New Mexico, was the home of a two-room school that now sits at the El Rancho de las Golondrinas, a two-hundred-acre "outdoor living museum." The school was originally located along the old Santa Fe Trail and served as a stop for the Atchison, Topeka and Santa Fe Railway.

The outdoor museum features not only the Raton schoolhouse but also a blacksmith shop, church, gristmill, and other structures built during the Spanish occupation. Two rooms of the original schoolhouse included a classroom plus an adjoining room where the teacher lived.

Photograph of the painting *The Old Santa Fe Trail* by Frederic Remington, depicting horsemen guiding a chain of ox-drawn carriages. Digitally reproduced by the USC Digital Library.
FROM THE CALIFORNIA HISTORICAL SOCIETY COLLECTION AT THE UNIVERSITY OF SOUTHERN CALIFORNIA

In 1885, Larson and his wife, Belle, began teaching deaf students in a small adobe house in Santa Fe. Using their own money, the deaf couple worked to develop and establish a permanent school where deaf and hard of hearing children could receive an education. In 1887, the New Mexico Legislature established the New Mexico School for the Deaf (NMSD). As documented by the school's own history, this school is the only land-grant school established for deaf students in the United States. Even today the school provides free admission to all students. According to the school's website, "We continue to honor Lars Larson's legacy by providing comprehensive educational and support services to New Mexico's deaf and hard of hearing children and youth between the ages of birth and 21."

A government-run Navajo Indian school was built in Tohatchi, in McKinley County, New Mexico, in 1901. It was a large one-story brick building. There was a round stone and a tall water tank to one side of the school.

According to Fr. John Mittelstadt, in a document he prepared for the seventy-fifth anniversary of the Tohatchi parish, "Tohatchi is a Navajo word meaning 'where the water is scratched out.'" However, according to Erik Painter,

> *Tohatchi is not a Navajo word, but an American English approximation of two Navajo words:* Tó Haach'i' Tó *means water and* haach'i' *is an obscure and archaic word that may be connected with* haachaii' *(he let out a cry)—perhaps referring to some long-ago incident.* Haach'i' *might also mean "It is customarily scratched out," referring to the high water level in Tohatchi Wash where a hole dug with your hands quickly fills with water.*

Tohatchi government school for Navajo on hill. Digitally reproduced by the USC Digital Library.
FROM THE CALIFORNIA HISTORICAL SOCIETY COLLECTION AT THE UNIVERSITY OF SOUTHERN CALIFORNIA

The Old Brazito

The Old Brazito ("Little Arm") Schoolhouse, built in 1916, was on the site of a little-known battle fought during the US war with Mexico, called the Battle of Brazito. It was the only battle fought in New Mexico during the Mexican-American War, and was precipitated when President James Polk ordered Colonel Stephen W. Kearny to seize New Mexico and protect American traders traveling to Santa Fe.

On Christmas Day, 1846, the Missouri Mounted Volunteers, totaling 850 men and commanded by Colonel Alexander Doniphan, made camp at the place called Brazito on the east bank of the Rio Grande. Having been given a day off for Christmas, the Americans were surprised by the Mexican Army (with seven hundred to one thousand men), led by General Antonio Ponce de Leon.

As related to the history of the Old Brazito' Schoolhouse, it was written: "In 1916, the land on which the battle had taken place was donated by F. M. Gallagher for the purpose of building a school. The one stipulation was that if the school was disbanded the land would return to Gallagher's heirs.

"Classes were held from 1916 to 1939 and then the land was returned to Gallagher's sole heir. In 1954, the land was purchased by the people of Brazito, but was sold once more in 1984. Finally in 2000, George Lee Carver purchased the property and restored the old school to its original condition."

The site was chosen by the Bureau of Indian Affairs for the second boarding school for the Navajo in 1895. In 1914, twenty-five children were enrolled in the boarding school.

The Ojo Sarco one-room school was located in an isolated mountainous community, and had eight grades and two teachers. As with so many schools in this region, the teachers had little equipment with which to work, so schoolwork was often completed on the blackboard.

NORTH DAKOTA

After the Dakota Territory was organized by Congress, and on the heels of the Homestead Act of 1862, settlement of the Dakotas began in earnest. A second surge in immigration occurred when the Western Pacific Railroad began laying track westward in 1872 and 1873. In the still sparsely settled Dakota Territory, however, one-room schoolhouses were a logical solution to the problem of few or poor roads and scattered communities and homesteads found throughout the Northern Plains. Small schools, sometimes called "country schools" (vs. "town schools"), were set up about every three miles, so that children were within a reasonable walking or horseback-riding distance. In addition, many of these early schools were made of sod since lumber or other building materials were hard to come by.

The first school building in North Dakota was built in Pembina, North Dakota, which is also the state's oldest town. The school operated from 1875 to 1881.

Across the state, the quality of education varied from one rural school to the next. To top it off, segregation and the lack of understanding seriously diminished the education that the region's Native American students received. Most Native American students attended schools established by missionaries on the reservations.

However, by the time the territory was officially split into two states in November 1889, there were no public high schools.

Even as the new states worked to certify teachers, most of them were only young girls with little education, some as young as fifteen or even fourteen.

Young Floyd Henderson taught school in Melby, North Dakota, in 1914, after obtaining special permission to teach from the Dunn County superintendent of schools because of a teacher shortage—even though he was technically too young to take a classroom. Following his hiring, in 1915, Henderson attended Valley City Normal School to pursue his certification.

🔔

The first school in the Northern Dakota Territory opened in Bismarck in 1873.

An overview of Bismarck, North Dakota's main street
DIGITALLY REPRODUCED BY THE USC DIGITAL LIBRARY. FROM THE CALIFORNIA HISTORICAL SOCIETY COLLECTION AT THE UNIVERSITY OF SOUTHERN CALIFORNIA

🔔

Born in Litchville, North Dakota, in 1897, Fred George Aandahl, North Dakota's twenty-third governor, attended a one-room country school there. It was a wood-frame building built in 1903 and torn down in 1924. In 1924, it was replaced by a three-story brick building with an imposing bell tower.

The Alderman School District #78 in Jamestown, North Dakota, was built in 1925–26. Eleven miles from Valley City, on County Route 21, it served as a one-room rural school from 1928 until 1959. In nearly original condition, the school was listed on the National Register of Historic Places on June 25, 2013.

Other towns in North Dakota to construct one-room schools included Aneta, Binford, Bisbee, Fargo, Hannaford, Harwood, Horace, Jamestown, Kenmare, Kulm, Lakota, Larimore, Mayville-Portland, Minto, Montpelier, Oriska, Page, Park River, Sherwood, and Wyndmere.

The Sweet Briar School, in Sweet Briar, was constructed in the mid-1920s. It was built by workers from the WPA (Works Progress Administration, created by President Roosevelt's New Deal Program) within the state. The school was located in the midst of low rolling hills, where few trees grew, and was unique in its Art Deco styling.

Fargo is the most populated community in North Dakota. Its first school was held in 1872, presumably in a log cabin. The first teacher was Miss Mercy Nelson, and she was only fifteen years old. The second school was held in a hall owned by Francis (Frank) Pinkham. The teacher was his sister, Miss Alvira Pinkham. These early schools were funded by subscription.

In September 1874, the citizens voted to build a public schoolhouse, on a lot provided by the Northern Pacific Railroad. The winter and summer terms were each three months long. As enrollment continued to grow, a second building was constructed. Still later, the school was remodeled and two more rooms were added.

By 1896, there were five public schools in Fargo. Until the students were given the opportunity to name their schools, these five schools were numbered. Eventually, the names of four of the five schools were selected: Washington, Lincoln, Longfellow, and Hawthorne. In 1909, three more schools were constructed: Roosevelt, McKinley, and the Douglas Terrace School.

Missouri Ridge Township was in Williams County. Kayann Short shared that her grand-mother Smith was a teacher in the local school. In the photos that follow, she noted that both of her grandfathers are in each. She wrote, "Both grandfathers were full of mischief. The school they attended was called Rocky Ridge, in Section 36 of Missouri Ridge Town-ship. Grandpa Smith was born in 1904 and Grandpa Short in 1908."

She continued, "In the photo of the barn, my grandfather is the darker-haired boy standing and waving his cap. In the second photo, the boys are, from left to right: Howard Short, my great-uncle; Kermit Smith, my maternal grandfather; a neighbor boy; Russell Short, my paternal grandfather; and another neighbor boy."

A Christmas school gathering in the snow at Missouri Ridge Township, North Dakota. Melissa Huns-ley, Kayann Short's great-great-grandmother (wearing black hood) stands at the right of the photo. Kayann's great-grandmother Short is to the right of her, along with Kayann's grandfather Russell in front. Note: the children are holding Christmas stockings after their school program.
COURTESY KAYANN SHORT

The boys built the barn where they could keep their horses while at school, circa the late 1910s.
COURTESY KAYANN SHORT

The boys are standing alongside the schoolhouse.
COURTESY KAYANN SHORT

Elaine Goodale Eastman

Elaine Goodale Eastman, born in 1863, was a novelist, poet, journalist, editor, activist, and a schoolteacher. She was born into a progressive and literary New England farm family. When the farm was sold and Elaine needed a job, she decided to teach.

After the Civil War, reformers and educators promoted the education of former slaves as well as Native Americans in the belief that they could "civilize" non-white peoples. At this time, Indian children were sent to off-reservation boarding schools in order to separate them from their cultures and teach them the ways of white society.

After Eastman took a job in the Indian Department at Hampton Institute in Virginia, she moved west to Dakota Territory. She opened a day school on a Sioux reservation, which she hoped would serve as a model for educating Indian children. By 1890, she had become the supervisor of Indian education for the territory, which by then had become North Dakota and South Dakota. In that role, she fought against the practice of removing Native American children from their families and sending them to distant boarding schools. She believed that the local day schools were the tool to "lift up" the entire community through assimilation. Most strikingly, though she loved the Sioux and their culture, she feared that if Native people failed to assimilate, they would be annihilated.

Elaine Goodale Eastman started a day school on a Dakota reservation in 1886.
COURTESY WIKIPEDIA

Elaine met Charles Eastman (Ohiyesa), a Santee Sioux who had been educated at Dartmouth and received a medical degree from Boston University. They married, but the marriage was not a happy one. Still, her advocacy for improving the lives of Native Americans continued.

While her values may seem contradictory to those expressed today, Elaine Goodman Eastman exerted a tremendous influence on the importance and relevance of nineteenth-century Native American education.

The Presentation Sisters Orphanage and School

The Presentation Sisters opened up St. John's Orphanage and Free School in Fargo, North Dakota, on September 8, 1897. The building had actually been the facility used by St. Joseph's Convent and Academy until those students were moved to the new Sacred Heart Academy. On January 19, 1907, the original wooden frame structure in which the school and orphanage had been housed was destroyed by fire. On Christmas Day, 1907, the new brick building for the orphanage was completed and dedicated. Eighty-seven students were enrolled on opening day. The four-story, brick and stone building cost $40,000.

As time went on, fewer orphans were enrolled and the facility began to decline. In 1958, the school was too deteriorated to maintain, and the Sisters constructed a new facility where they could care for emotionally disturbed children as well as the homeless.

OKLAHOMA

The county seat of Cherokee County, Tahlequah, lies in the eastern section of Oklahoma only thirty miles from the Arkansas state line. Established as the Cherokee capital by the Cherokee people in 1839, the town became a prosperous and cohesive community. The Cherokee were a progressive people, and the community grew around the town square.

By 1842, Tahlequah had four stores and a thriving business community. The great Indian Intertribal Council of 1843 brought an influx of ten thousand people, with twenty-one tribes represented. The first school opened in 1845 and even a concept of higher education became a reality when the Cherokee Male and Female Seminaries were opened in 1851.

The Cherokee Female Seminary, built at Park Hill, Oklahoma, burned in 1887, but was rebuilt in Tahlequah. It then became Northeastern State Normal School and then Northeastern State Teachers College (now Northeastern State University).

Western expansion reached Oklahoma in the late 1800s. In 1889, a portion of the open land that became known as Indian Territory was opened to white settlement, and those who were able to were offered an opportunity to join in various land races. At this point, the early pioneers to Oklahoma Territory had to make do with what they could bring or build on their own.

The first arrivals came in covered wagons and brought few or no luxuries.

Homes at first were crude, built of raw timber or sod. It was hard to keep them warm in winter, and during the summer, flies and fleas swarmed "like armies." Windows were square holes cut out of hewn logs, occasionally covered with greased paper.

Such was W. J. Milburn's early life, as shared by Lynn Milburn Lansford in her book *Milburn: The Birth of a Pioneer Town and the Love Story that Began There.*

W. J. himself wrote (in 1953), that in 1887, "when a boy of 16, I crossed Red River in a wagon between Gainesville, Texas, and Thackerville, Indian Territory, and drove as far northeast as a sulphur spring where there were at that time no houses, but a tent in which a man lived and kept a few groceries for sale. We paid him 10 cents a pound for flour, filled our jug with sulphur water and turned back towards Texas."

W. J. Milburn continued, "Later that year we drove about 125 miles east into the Chickasaw country and located at the little village of Emet near where I was to teach a subscription school at $1.00 per pupil per month. Teachers were not required to secure a license, certification, or diploma. Neither were doctors or dentists, also druggists taught or practiced without a license. In fact, there were no examining boards to grant licenses. Pupils attended my school to study their A B Cs, reading, spelling, arithmetic, geography, history, and algebra. No grades, but each student progressed as fast as he and the teacher working together made possible. . . . On the trip to Emet, we did not have a mile of public road, a bridge or free ferry. The only railroad we saw was at Ardmore, a small but growing town which had sprung up as the result of the building of the Santa Fe across the Chickasaw country from Kansas to Texas."

Alma Jane (Son) Milburn also wrote about her life in Lynn Milburn Lansford's book. Born in 1891, she and her family lived in various places in Missouri before moving to Indian Territory when she was just ten years old. Because her grandmother was one-eighth Indian they hoped to "get property." Though the entire Son family charted a Pullman train to go to Indian Territory together, they did not succeed in getting any promised property.

Alma did relate a story about attending school: "All of the kids walked to Overbrook to school. It was two miles. We went to that school for three years. As I think of it now, we are all lucky to be alive because we walked that distance to school down the Santa Fe Railroad track. . . . The railroad track ran north and south.

"One morning in the springtime we were walking to school down the railroad track. It was a very windy day. The wind was blowing from the south. Something made one of the children suddenly look around and there was a train almost on us! The train was whistling madly, but we couldn't hear it because of the wind. We all jumped off the track, just in time!"

Reportedly, Oklahoma had 3,638 one-teacher/one-room schools, beginning in the 1890s. Today the Rose Hill School in Perry (built in 1895) and the Pleasant Valley School in Stillwater operate living history programs for students. The Verden Separate School—which served African-American students near Chickasha—and the Turkey Creek School—now in the Humphrey Heritage Village at the Cherokee Strip Regional Heritage Center in Enid, Oklahoma—are also open to visitors.

🔔

Loretta Jackson, the founder of the Loretta Y. Jackson Historical Society, was responsible for saving the one-room Verden Separate School from demolition. She also organized the one-hundredth-year anniversary commemoration of that school. The Verden School purchased a CSAA Landmark Schoolhouse plaque documenting its acceptance into the Country School Association of America National Schoolhouse Registry.

🔔

The coming of the Chicago, Rock Island and Pacific Railroad in 1888 to nearby Liberal, Kansas, as well as the coming of other railroad lines, actually helped draw more settlers to Oklahoma. As new railroad towns built businesses along the track—including banks, stores, and lumberyards—they also constructed schools. By the 1920s, there were fifty-three one-room schools in Beaver County alone.

🔔

Ash Grove School, or School #45 in Ash Grove, Comanche County, Oklahoma, operated for an eight-month term, beginning in September. The student population generally numbered between fifteen and twenty-two students.

When Oklahoma became a state, there were more than 5,500 schoolhouses and 257,000 school children. In 1907, the state constitution provided a policy regarding the adoption of a single textbook. As time went on, the state also worked to standardize rural schools—their construction as well as their curriculum. M. A. Nash, who was the state superintendent in 1922, instituted the Model School Score Card. In 1924, only five hundred schools qualified as model schools rated by their physical environments, including playground equipment, health and safety standards, even school organization and instructional equipment.

Helen Hussman Morris, who was born in 1910 near Fonda, Oklahoma, taught between 1929 and 1935. In a biography written by her daughter, it is clear that Helen

Ash Grove School, Oklahoma
COURTESY LEWIS WICKES HINE, PHOTOGRAPHER/ LIBRARY OF CONGRESS

loved her job but at times faced a number of challenges; however, she learned to persevere and overcome.

As a junior in high school, Helen began to substitute teach for absent teachers, and then she was asked to take over a first grade class. In 1929, as a senior, she decided to take the two-day exam that would qualify her to teach for one or two years. After passing the exam, she was offered a job by the Orion school board. The Orion school was located in a canyon; it was a simple clapboard school, built in 1895, but much more primitive than Helen had realized it would be.

In contrast to many of the methods employed by teachers of the day, Helen resisted punishing her students too harshly. "The pupils had told her about the punishments used by the previous teachers: spanking with a yardstick, ruler or switch; standing in the corner; standing with the pupil's nose in a circle on the blackboard; staying under the teacher's desk; and standing on the floor (standing on a raised platform near the teacher's desk)."

OREGON

In the 1850s, when the first public schools were formed in Portland, Oregon, free public education was still a new concept. On December 6, 1851, the following advertisement appeared in *The Oregonian*:

> *In pursuance of a vote of the Portland school district at their annual meeting, the directors have established a free school. The first term will commence on Monday, the 15th inst., at the schoolhouse in this city, near the City Hotel (John W. Outhouse, teacher). The directors would recommend the following books to be used in the school, viz.:* Sandler's Series of Readers and Spellers, Goodrich's Geography, Thompson's Arithmetics and Bullion's Grammar.

John Outhouse, the school's first teacher, was paid $100 a month. There were only twenty students. By the third term, however, the population rose to 126 students—with ninety as the daily average attendance. A second teacher was hired, Miss Abigail Clarke. She was paid $75 a month. It was said that Miss Clarke often chided "the boys who were known to 'make sport' by tapping on the windows."

In December 1854, with more students seeking an education, Portland's school board organized two districts: School District #1 and School District #2. Then, in March 1856, the two districts merged into one. A new schoolhouse was built in 1858.

The Oregon State Constitution of 1859 established a system of common schools. It also appointed the governor to serve as superintendent of public instruction with the instructions that after five years the Legislative Assembly would create an independent office to oversee the state's educational system.

Today Oregon is home to more frontier ghost towns than any other state in the nation. In these and many other locations are the remains of dozens of historic schoolhouses. At least twenty-six Oregon pioneer schoolhouses are still standing. A handful of these include Lost Creek in Benton County, Center Ridge in Wasco County, Braunsport in Columbia County, Yoder (a Mennonite school) in Clackamas County, and Howard School in Ochoco.

🔔

A log cabin, built circa 1856, in the Alsea Valley, Benton County, Oregon, was the site of the first school there. The school was moved around, but in 1909, two schools joined to form a consolidated school district. Both burned in 1930, so a single new school was built, but that school also burned in 1949. Another school was then constructed.

Lone Pine School

Hugh and Denis O'Connor emigrated from Ireland in 1907. They came to Lake County, Oregon, where they joined two other brothers who had already immigrated. They got jobs in a sheep camp, but Hugh left to work in San Francisco for six months before rejoining Denis, who was herding sheep on the open range.

Within four years they had an interest in several hundred sheep, and by 1918, their operation covered 800 acres in Lake County; they also owned land near Bonanza, Rock Creek, and Stukel Mountain. The O'Connors raised three thousand lambs a year, as well as alfalfa, hay, grain, and potatoes. In 1923, Hugh married Miss Marie Dolan, a schoolteacher who had boarded at the brothers' large house while teaching at the Lone Pine School.

🔔

Kings Valley School was founded in 1848. Located twenty miles northwest of Corvallis, Oregon, it is likely the oldest rural district still in operation in Benton County. The first structure was a log building; the second, built circa 1860, was a frame building, first painted red, then painted white.

In 1892, a new school was built, located at the junction of Kings Valley Highway and Maxfield Creek Road. By 1914, a high school wing was added. The school, which now serves kindergarten through fourth grade, has been in existence for more than 160 years.

🔔

Located eight miles north of Corvallis, Oregon, sits the one-room Soap Creek School. The school was built in 1935, during the Great Depression. It was the third school to be built on the site.

Pete Johannsen built the school and it is believed that some of the building's elements, such as the window casings, are probably older than the 1930s, perhaps from an earlier structure. The narrow protected valley was homesteaded in the 1840s and some records indicate that the Soap Creek School was the earliest one established in Benton County. One former attendee suggested that the first school might have been built around 1885.

Charles Olson attended the school, beginning in 1904, and story has it that one day a boy—who was apparently in trouble quite often—"was standing by the stove drying his clothes when the teacher asked him to move so she could put more wood in the stove, which had a lid that swung out horizontally on a hinge. He rudely ignored her, so, perhaps in exasperation, she swung the lid around anyway. It caught him right behind the knees causing him to sit on the hot stove lid with a definite 'sizzle.'"

Olson told another story about something that occurred when he was twelve or thirteen. Because he and his sister had to tromp through heavily wooded areas where wild animals often roamed, he carried a pistol; he hid it in the woodshed behind the school so the teacher wouldn't find it. However, one day he stopped to talk to his uncle on his way home and his sister walked on. When he finally got home she told him that a large coyote had confronted her, but "she stood her ground until it leaped into the underbrush."

When a large timber wolf was killed some time later, Olson and his sister wondered if she'd actually come face-to-face with a wolf.

The school districts in Linn County were organized circa 1854, and Rock Hill School District was one of them. The first schoolhouse was built of logs and may have been built before 1853. Many early schools were one-room log buildings. Rock Hill School is located four and one-half miles south of Lebanon, Oregon.

Possibly fifty or more pupils crowded into the small log school, and many lessons were completed through recitation and repetition. One student reported, "We sat on slab benches which were without backs. Each bench was about ten feet long and there were no desks."

Oak Grove School was built in 1860 and is located west of Albany, Oregon, in farmland among the rolling hills. The school burned between 1888 and 1893, and the school's replacement was a large white house. Today the school is part of the Greater Albany School District.

The present Rock Hill schoolhouse is the last of five separate structures built; however, records indicate that it may be the oldest of nine schoolhouses in Linn County that are still standing on their original sites. According to Elaine Hart, who wrote about the history of the Rock Hill school for the Linn County School District Rock Hill School History, "The present school building was constructed between 1895 and 1905, but there were four other buildings before. The first building was constructed in 1853 as a log cabin, and the students sat on slab benches without backs. It was destroyed by fire, probably in the late 1860s. The second schoolhouse was an old church building where camp meetings had been held. The third building was intended to be a church building, and was constructed by the Church of the United Brethren in Christ." It was a frame building begun by the United Brethren Church on an acre of land purchased from William and Lydia Gallaher, but construction was halted temporarily because the church ran out of money. William Gallaher had been the original school's first teacher. Construction resumed when the school committee joined forces with the church.

From the beginning, the Rock Hill School maintained a close relationship with the Church of the United Brethren in Christ. The United Brethren Church believed in a strong, formal education, even admitting women into colleges in the early 1800s, followed by admitting African Americans to Otterbein College in Ohio. Interestingly, the college president's home was a station on the Underground Railroad, which helped slaves escape. Even today, according to the church's website, "We believe that we are educating the leaders of tomorrow and we want those leaders to look to God for guidance in their decision making. Proverbs 22:6 tells us 'Train a child in the way he should go, and when he is old he will not turn from it'."

Late in the spring of 1935, the doors of Rock Hill School closed. In November 1960, the Linn County School District sold the schoolhouse and its surrounding acreage to Norma and Gilbert Morgan for $206. Then, in March 1986, the Linn County Historic Resource Commission placed the structure on the Linn County Historic Register. Finally, in April 1991, thirteen citizens met to develop plans for preserving the structure, and the Rock Hill School Foundation was formed.

Most of Rock Hill's early teachers were men, including "Old Man" Gallaher, also known as James Jackson Gallaher (a one-armed teacher who lost his arm in a threshing accident). Another was W. R. Bishop, who taught from 1856 through 1861. And there was James Knox Polk Weatherford, who was elected Linn County school superintendent in 1874. Weatherford also passed the bar in 1875, served in the State Legislature in 1876, and in 1884 became a state senator.

The school in Denny, Oregon, built in the 1880s, was named for Owen Denny, who brought ring-necked pheasants to Oregon after serving as the US Consul in China. These Denny School children pose with their sign in November 1919.

Gold Beach, on the Oregon coast, was originally named Ellensburg after settlers who arrived in the 1850s, and the Ellensburg post office was established in 1853. Local miners began to call it "Gold Beach" after gold was discovered in the sands at the mouth of Rogue River, although the amount recovered did not live up to the high hopes of those who rushed to the site.

As settlers moved in on the heels of the miners, a number of battles between the Rogue River Indians and the newcomers took place. The conflicts, referred to as the Rogue River Wars, occurred from 1855 to 1856 and involved the US Army, local militias and volunteers, and local tribes. After the tribes were defeated, the Tillamook, Siletz, and about twenty other tribes were displaced and forced, along with the Tolowa, onto the Siletz and Grande Ronde Reservations.

In 1858, Gold Beach became the county seat of Curry County. From Gold Beach, boats were used to deliver mail up and down the Rogue River. Today the Rogue River mail boat service remains one of only two rural boat services in the country.

ONE ROOM

🔔

Talent, in Jackson County, Oregon, is located between Ashland and Medford. It sits at the confluences of Wagner and Anderson Creeks and Bear Creek. Jacob Wagner filed the first land claim in 1852 and for a time, Talent was known as Wagner Creek.

The first schoolhouse was built along Bear Creek circa 1854, but that school, along with a second—and possibly a third—no longer exist. In 1899, the Talent Elementary School was built near downtown. It is a one-story, wood-frame, classically designed structure, with a bell tower. In 1914, it was converted into the town hall. Today the old schoolhouse has retained its original design, although it is used as a community center.

🔔

While Irene Bennett Brown, an author of children's, young adult, and adult fiction, was born in Kansas, she and her family moved to the Willamette Valley in Oregon when she was nine years old. She attended the one-room school known as Diamond Hill located in the Cascade Foothills. Diamond Hill, for which the school was named, rises up behind the simple wood-framed structure.

Ms. Brown noted that she was the only student in the fifth grade and one of eleven students in the first-through-eighth-grade country school. The teacher was provided a room "in the loft of a shed on a nearby farmer's property."

🔔

Shaniko, in Wasco County, Oregon, is one of the most photographed schools in Oregon. The town's history is equally as interesting. Originally it was the site of the Cross Hollows Stage Station and Post Office, run by August Scherneckau, a German immigrant. Because the local tribe—with whom Herr Scherneckau had developed a relationship—could not pronounce his name, they called him Shaniko. When a branch of the Columbia Southern Railway was laid to the old station to transport wool produced by local sheepherders, a new post office was established and called Shaniko.

The town grew quickly. A large, two-story brick hotel was built, complete with heat in every room. A fancy two-story firehouse was also built.

The schoolhouse was built at the north edge of town in 1902. Uniquely designed, it boasted a tall, octagonal entry and bell tower. The building was large and square and its roof slanted from all sides up to a flat top.

Today, Shaniko is only a shadow of a town, although the size and dimensions of the town's water tower, along with the size and architecture of the school, are clues about the town's early success.

🔔

On the last day of May 1871, the Logtown School District was established in the Applegate Valley in southern Oregon. An earlier schoolhouse had been built of local rough-hewn wood, with handmade benches. In 1876, mostly through the influence of Martin Drake, a new frame school was built, called the Drake School.

In 1897, the district was re-designated the Ruch District. By 1912, the school was deteriorating, and the school board approved a bond to finance a new school. The dilapidated frame building was dismantled, slat by slat, and the materials reused for other buildings. A more substantial schoolhouse was dedicated in May 1914. In 2014, it celebrated its one hundredth anniversary.

The new school featured a bell tower. Two years later a high school was added to the school, but it survived only two years—perhaps because so many of the area's young men enlisted in World War I.

🔔

Located along Highway 66, east of Ashland, Oregon—locally known as the Greensprings highway—is the Pinehurst School. In the mid-1800s, emigrant wagon trains traveled through this wooded area where they had to negotiate the "Jenny Creek Slide," a steep hill where wagons were lowered while tied to trees, which held them steady and upright.

Aleatha Slater was one early resident who shared her family's story in the book *Pinehurst School: 100 Years of Growing up on the Greensprings*, compiled by locals and organized by Sam Alvord. Aleatha's grandfather, George Washington Riley Bailey, took up land grant property on Jenny Creek. There he built a shake mill and made shakes, shingles, posts, and rails. The family's log house soon became the first post office and a stagecoach stop between Ashland and Klamath Falls, known as Shake.

In 1908, local residents—led by Charles DeCarlow, Fred Edsall, and Bill Cox—joined together to create the Jackson County School District #94; the district was also named Shake. Located on Beaver Creek, just one hundred feet from where the Ashland-Klamath Falls stage road crossed the creek, the school was built by locals. In 1911, the school district was renamed Pinehurst when Lulu DeCarlow, postmistress, petitioned to change it. The first school was replaced five years later, while the second schoolhouse served the community until 1920. Today the school continues to thrive.

A few important individuals in the history of Pinehurst included Bob and Flora Willis, who ran the school from 1951 through 1967, and Laurie Grupé, who spent thirty years as head teacher.

Other early schools in the extended region included Plush, Paisley, Frenchglen, and Diamond.

Children first attended classes at the one-room Criterion School in Wasco County, Oregon, in 1912, where it sat on the high desert near Maupin. Although the school ceased to operate in 1925, the building remained a community resource, used as a Sunday school, a dance hall, a voting space, and a location for other public events.

In 1953, the building closed and sat vacant for over twenty years. Then, in 1976, the Criterion Schoolhouse began a new life, including a two-hundred-mile journey to the

Criterion School ceased to operate in 1925.
COURTESY GAIL L. JENNER COLLECTION

Oregon State Fairgrounds. The school was chosen from a group of more than fifty schools in Oregon to serve as an exhibit for the nation's Bicentennial Celebration.

🔔

In 1906, Miss Ina Stocker and her mother moved to Jackson County from Iowa where she had taught school. Ina took a teaching job at Beaver Creek School in the Applegate Valley. In 1908, she met and married Nelson Pursel. The couple eventually moved to the Yale Creek area.

Reportedly Ina rode to school each day on horseback. She chopped wood to keep the fire going in the classroom's small wood stove, and—ever enterprising—she occasionally pulled several students across the Applegate River in a trolley to get them to school. Ina Stocker Pursel taught for more than fifty years, forty of them in small schools. She retired in 1958. At age ninety-three, she passed away and was buried beside her husband in the Jacksonville Cemetery.

🔔

Medford, in Jackson County, Oregon, was founded in 1883 when the railroad came to southern Oregon. Enthusiasm for the budding community surged and, as noted on its city webpage sponsored by the Medford Landmarks & Historic Preservation Commission, "During that first year several babies were born, a fatal shoot-out took place, the first of many churches organized, a schoolhouse was built, and trains began shuttling freight and passengers to Portland. As if to say 'we have arrived,' Medford's citizens brashly hosted a Fourth of July gala for the whole Rogue Valley."

The first school was a one-room schoolhouse on South Central Avenue. It was a subscription school and cost $5 for each student to attend. The school's first teacher was William A. Williamson. The next year, a parcel of land was purchased from C. C. Beekman, and the city built its second school. It was a wood-frame two-story structure; its first principal was Walter Gore and there were three primary teachers: May Crain, Belle Stronk, and Sophia Wilson. As the school grew, more teachers were hired to teach the upper grades. In 1891, the school was moved to West Tenth Street.

By the early 1900s, agriculture and commercial fruit had become the area's major industry, and Medford became one of the fastest growing cities in the United States. Today Medford's school district is the largest in southern Oregon.

Henry Clay Tison arrived in southern Oregon with his wife and eight children in August 1897. After settling in the town of Drew, twenty-nine miles east of Canyonville, Tison, along with his neighbors, built a one-room schoolhouse in 1906. Miss Carrie Anderson was Tison's first schoolteacher and she married Henry Tison Jr., in 1919. Today the school remains the only known hand-hewn log schoolhouse in Douglas County and serves as the Drew Museum.

Nancy Fine also wrote about Harney County's rural schools: "In Harney County, in eastern Oregon, there are seven rural schools, [and most,] like Pine Creek and others, are one-room; [that is,] instruction takes place in one room although there may be a library, kitchen or gym, etc. One of the schools has a whopping two students registered!"

Nancy stated, "My husband, now sixty-six, attended one of these schools—Frenchglen Elementary. We call them 'rural schools' because in town—Burns and Hines—there is a high school, junior high, and elementary school. The rest are out of town, hence rural. . . . Remote is more like it. We are designated a frontier county due to our 'in-the-sticks' status. Harney County is ten thousand square miles with around seven thousand people."

Nancy went on to share: "Another interesting district is Crane, also in Harney County. There, grades [kindergarten] through twelve are all on 'one piece of dirt.' [Obviously] to have a public boarding high school is a rarity itself nowadays. The boarding school is in place so the 'waaay-out-of-town' kids, such as ranch kids or the students from Fields, which is 102 miles from Crane, aren't [traveling] for impossibly long bus rides. . . . travel from some areas can be delayed due to drifting snow on highways in winter or dirt roads and mud in spring. There's an expression here, which is, 'Wait for the road to tighten up'—meaning wait for the road to freeze so the mud doesn't swallow up you and your rig."

In 1867, William Brown, a shoemaker and one of two hundred African-American Oregonians living in Portland, sued the school district for refusing to educate the sixteen black children residing in the city. In response, the "Colored School" opened in the fall of 1867, but was discontinued in 1872 when a referendum supported integration. By December 1873, thirty students out of 1,048 within the district were black.

Schools for African-American students were rarely provided the same materials or financial attention that schools for white children were given.
COURTESY GAIL L. JENNER COLLECTION

By the end of the 1870s, there were four elementary schools in the Portland area: Central School (1858–?), Harrison School (1866–?); the "Colored School" of Portland (1867–1872), and North School (1868–?). The cost to educate a student in 1879 in Portland was $24.06.

Linda Jones Weber shared that she attended a two-room schoolhouse in Garden Valley, Oregon, five miles from Roseburg, in the Umpqua Valley. It was called Riversdale and there were four grades in each room, first through fourth and fifth through eighth.

According to Linda, "I started there in second grade, in 1951, and my teacher was Sally Rapp. My third grade teacher was Mrs. Cook and she was Native American. In the fourth grade, the 'school library' was a set of three shelves under the windows next to my desk. I became fascinated with books and read every single book in the library." She continued, "We had both indoor plumbing and outhouses. One day the plumbing broke so we all had to use the outhouses. Three of us came down with polio that weekend, and I was one of the unlucky ones. By the time I reached fifth grade, we had been absorbed into the Roseburg School District. But that little two-room school was the center of our rural universe."

The one-room schoolhouse in Oakland, Oregon, in Douglas County, was most likely built circa 1910 to replace an earlier school. According to historian Larry Moulton, who compiled a book on Douglas County school history, the first school for the early "English Settlement" community was built of hand-hewn timbers or logs in 1854 or 1855. That first building was located one mile to the south of Oakland, on Oldham Creek.

Other settlers to the area, particularly emigrating Americans, began arriving in the second half of the 1840s and 1850s, spurred on by the opening of the Applegate Trail in 1846. Although not incorporated for many years, towns such as Oakland and others, including Wilbur, Winchester, and Drain, were early communities in Douglas County.

The Oakland school was a rectangular, one-story, wood-frame, one-room schoolhouse set on a foundation of basalt. The interior consisted of a single room with a small foyer and two cloak rooms, finished with beadboard wainscoting. Electric lights and other accommodations were added later on.

Located on Elkhead Road in rural Douglas County, the old schoolhouse sat eight miles northeast of the city of Oakland, in a ravine between rolling hills. In order to preserve it, the foundation along the north and west sides was replaced with lumber and concrete footings.

Last used as a school around 1930, the building was left abandoned and vacant, and at times, used by animals for shelter. Then, in 2005, the Friends of Mildred Kanipe Memorial Park Association began cleaning up the school, and the Douglas County Parks Department removed the deteriorated siding, replaced rotten foundation joists, and placed the building on a new cement block foundation. However, several of the original foundation stones and much of the original foundation still support the building. The Oakland School was added to the National Register of Historic Places in 2007.

SOUTH DAKOTA

Across the plains, whether to the south or north, district sizes generally ran between two to four miles square, but in western South Dakota, districts were larger. General William Henry Harrison Beadle was the leader in establishing educational funding as a part of South Dakota's state constitution. A Civil War veteran, he served as the territorial superintendent of public instruction from 1879 to 1885. When South Dakota's constitution was drawn up, he proposed that the sixteenth and thirty-sixth section of each township be set aside for public school use.

By 1916, there were 5,011 one-room schools across the eighty thousand square miles representing the state of South Dakota. Often these schools also served as community halls or churches, where weddings and baptisms and funerals were held. At the Lame Johnny School in South Dakota, denominations gathered together for joint services on Sunday. In Kingsbury County, South Dakota, the Congregational Church met for twenty years in the Brown School, while the Bethel Mennonite Church in Marion met at the West Vermillion School from 1883 until 1892. Even during the Depression, hungry children looked forward to the noon meal served at school, although more than a thousand one-room schools closed in South Dakota during the Depression.

Conditions were met with resilience by those who settled across the state. As described by one teacher, Julia Hall, in *Memoirs of South Dakota Retired Teachers*, in 1976, "My bedroom was an unfinished attic room with an outside stairway which at times was slick with ice and snow . . . the room was heated with a small wood and coal stove. . . . I kept my clothes under the covers so they would be warm in the morning; sometimes my bed was covered with snow. I would go downstairs to wash, eat breakfast and take my school bag and pail to start walking the one and a half miles to school."

With regard to Native American education, South Dakota State Superintendent Charles H. Lugg reported in 1916, "The non-white population of the state is almost wholly Indian, and the illiterates among the Indians are still wards of the federal government for whom our schools are not responsible."

As in other states, Native American students attended boarding schools. Such schools required the boys to cut their hair, cropping it close to the scalp, while girls were made to wear tightly buttoned dresses that covered them from neckline to ankle. While 95 percent of the Native American students returned home to their families, they were caught between two worlds.

Some of these Indian schools were given unique names. For example, schools on the Pine Ridge reservation included Red Shirt Table, Wakpamini, Wounded Knee, Lone

Man, and Porcupine. On the Cheyenne River reservation, there were Red Scaffold, Bridger, Iron Lightning, Thunder Butte, Four Bear, Green Brass, Bear Creek, Moreau River, and White Horse Schools.

As boarding schools and missionary schools were replaced by day schools, a more serious attempt to keep students in their own communities began in the 1930s. During the Depression, teachers came from all over the country to teach at reservation schools. However, since most of the children spoke Lakota, and as few as two or three out of fifty students spoke English, communication between the pupils and English-speaking teachers was strained and sometimes impossible. Schoolbooks reflected a culture that was foreign. Discipline was difficult and attendance was erratic. For Native Americans, as well as for African-American children, school was often a frightening place. Moreover, minority schools lacked the materials afforded white school children.

With the coming of World War I, schools were also facing the ugly clouds of discrimination and fear against German and, in many places, Italian immigrants. Interestingly, in 1915, Supreme Court Justice Louis Brandeis gave a speech on "true Americanism." He stated, "He (the immigrant) must be brought into complete harmony with our ideals and aspirations and cooperate with us for their attainment. Only when this has been done will he possess the national consciousness of an American."

In 1919, South Dakota passed the Americanization Act, which required that all students between sixteen and twenty-one who could not speak or read or write in English attend day or night school. The state paid one-half the cost of instruction. Most ethnic groups complied, but a number resisted. The Hutterites, in retaliation, sold their lands and moved to Canada. They did not return for twenty years.

Country schools in South Dakota assisted in teaching immigrants. Michael M. Guhin established the Young Citizens League (YCL). He had reportedly borrowed the concept from a Minnesota education bulletin, *The Little Citizens League*. Hoping to encourage cultural assimilation and strong cultural values, he started a YCL chapter in Brown County while acting as county superintendent of schools. In 1919, Guhin was appointed state director of Americanization, under the direction of South Dakota's superintendent of public instruction.

While YCLs were created in neighboring states, the league remained most popular in South and North Dakota. Forty chapters were set up in Brown County alone by 1915. By 1927, YCL reported over 3,400 chapters, with over sixty thousand members. In 1925, South Dakota's superintendents voted to make YCL chapters mandatory for all public

The Old School at Volga, South Dakota
COURTESY GAIL L. JENNER COLLECTION

schools in the state. The groups sponsored projects and helped to bring improvements and innovations into the schools through volunteerism and fund-raising.

Evelyn Myers Sharping, a student at the Swanson School in Brule County in 1931, recalled her YCL experience in *One-Room Country School: South Dakota Stories*: "On bad days we played Hide the Thimble or games at the blackboard such as Cat and Hangman. . . . With our YCL money we bought a Carrom (a tabletop multiple game) board. We also purchased a Monopoly set. The game took so long that we would just leave it all set up and continue from where we had left off at the last recess."

The YCL "march song" became well known; the chorus included these words:

ONE ROOM

In all the winds of heaven
There breathes a patriot's creed...
Clean hearts and minds and bodies
Serve best our country's need

The YCL promoted patriotism as well as helped to establish moral and socially conscious citizens. With the decline of rural schools following World War II, YCL membership declined and eventually faded away.

School programs were an important part of life for the children and community alike. At Clark School, in Douglas County, South Dakota, the attendance at one school event was so thick that the gas lamps around the room would not burn because there was too little oxygen left in the room. Many children witnessed their first sight of a Christmas tree or Christmas decorations at school programs. Even when blizzards hit the plains, parents crowded into the schoolroom for such important events. Oftentimes whole families had to sleep on the floor of the school if the weather was too bad to make their way home.

Eleanore Rowan Moe, who attended the Rowan School in Sanborn County from 1926 to 1933, shared a Christmas story in *One-Room Country School: South Dakota Stories*, "How thrilling the Christmas tree was—towering far above our heads. It was so much larger than anyone had at home, its branches covered with REAL candles. . . . Our home Christmas tree was a huge tumbleweed which Mother covered with sparkling starch. We drew names for presents, but we exchanged names again and again to get the name we really wanted. Gradually packages were sneaked under the pine branches and candles were checked and double-checked for safety."

Another South Dakota student from Sanborn County, Gladys Brewick, shared her story: "Each lady (or girl) would decorate a box, usually a shoe box, and fill it with all sorts of goodies to eat. The identity of the box-maker was kept a secret. These boxes were auctioned off by some man from the neighborhood, and the money taken in would be used by the school for supplies, such as books, maps, gloves, and other things. . . . I must say, too, that every man who bought a box ate the lunch from that box with the girl or lady who brought it. The teacher's box usually sold for a good price!"

TEXAS

The Texas Declaration of Independence in 1836 listed the failure of the Mexican government "to establish any public system of education, although possessed of almost boundless resources" as one of the reasons for cutting ties with Mexico.

The first Anglo-American public school law in Texas was enacted in 1840 and provided for surveying and setting aside four leagues (17,712 acres) of land in each county to support public schools. Later, the state constitution of 1845 provided that one-tenth of the annual state tax revenue was to be set aside as a "perpetual fund" to support free public schools. After the Civil War and Reconstruction, the new state constitution of 1876 set aside 45 million acres of public domain for school support. In 1884, the school law was rewritten, and the Permanent School Fund was to be invested in county schools; other bonds followed to increase income.

According to Betty McCreary, of Austin, the Esperanza (which means "hope") School was one of the earliest one-room schoolhouses in Travis County, Texas, and was built on property provided by Richard McKenzie in 1866. It served rural children before public education was being provided.

In 1893, when a larger Esperanza School was built on another site, the old log structure was used for other things. The roughly constructed, hand-hewn school was later moved to the Pioneer Village in Austin's Zilker Botanical Garden. The original log structure received a Texas Historical Marker in 1974 and is furnished to look like a school might have in the 1860s or later.

The first school along the Pedernales River in Gillespie County was actually held in a tent, but in 1882, a new school, the Junction School, was built a mile down the road. Then in 1910, John Pehl donated property for a better school.

As a four-year-old living not far from the rural one-room Junction School in Gillespie County, Texas, the young Lyndon Baines Johnson liked to ride his horse and was often found outside the school, anxious to play with the school children. Then, as one of the youngest students, he recalled sitting in the lap of his teacher, Miss Katie Deadrich, as she read the day's reading lesson.

Johnson only attended Junction School for a few months in 1912 because the school had to be closed (temporarily) after an epidemic of whooping cough struck the area. The Johnson family moved away shortly after.

The Junction School was a typical one-room school with a wood stove as the only source of heat. Two kerosene lamps hung from the ceiling, and the children sat together at wooden desks, arranged in two rows, with boys in one row and girls in another. The school officially closed in 1947. In 1972, the National Park Foundation purchased the land to become part of the Lyndon B. Johnson National Historical Park.

Helotes, Texas, is home to a school named Los Reyes. From 1871 to 1939, local residents built three one-room schoolhouses. Each of the schools was given the name Los Reyes for the nearby Los Reyes Creek.

According to Helotes author and historian Cynthia Leal Massey, the original Los Reyes was the first school established in the area. Built in 1871, on property provided by Lorenzo Morales, the school was located off Bandera Road about four miles north of Scenic Loop Road.

The first Los Reyes school was replaced in 1882 with a one-room limestone structure built on land donated by Frank Madla, and located about two miles from the intersection of Bandera and Scenic Loop Roads. According to Armin Elmendorf, a former teacher at this Los Reyes schoolhouse, average attendance numbered only six to eight students, ranging in age from seven to twenty-two. Henry T. Brauchle taught at this Los Reyes from 1902 to 1906.

The third Los Reyes and a teacher's cottage were built in 1912, again on land donated by Frank Madla. The school's location, however, was convenient for students who either walked two to three miles to school or rode a horse, donkey, or pony.

This Los Reyes schoolhouse was constructed of wood and considered a more modern structure than the previous Los Reyes schools. Although it didn't have indoor plumbing or electricity (at least initially), it did have a well, separate outhouses (one for boys and one for girls), plus chalkboards, and a wood-burning heater.

The one-room Helotes School, circa 1908. Fred Wendt's mother is in the photo (not identified).
COURTESY FRED WENDT

In 1939, school trustees decided to merge Los Reyes with the Helotes School; both schools were moved to land donated by Kate and James Riggs, and a third classroom was built that connected the two schools. Today, this school is known as the Helotes Elementary School and is still located on Riggs Road. Both of these schools—Los Reyes and Helotes—represent two of the twelve pioneer schools in the area that were finally consolidated in 1949.

Riding out for a picnic on horseback; note the lunch baskets, hats, and book bags tied onto the saddles. Again, the one-room Helotes School, circa 1908.
COURTESY FRED WENDT

Another early school in Texas was the Clifton (or Clifden) School on Bandera Road in the northeast tip of Medina County. According to early records, Clifden was a planned community that never materialized. It had a post office and a school. From 1884 to 1914, children attended a one-room wooden structure. Mr. John Coleman was the teacher.

In 1914, August D. Schott moved the first Clifton School onto his ranch in Bexar County, which is today the fourth largest county in Texas. The first teacher was Mrs. Euchle, and a series of teachers taught until 1932, when the school burned down.

While planning to build a new facility, a temporary Clifton School was set up in a large metal barn located on the Logan Ranch at the southeast edge of San Geronimo. It was noted that inside the barn there is an "interesting forked center post, where carved hearts and initials of past students, are still visible."

The new Clifton School was built on the same site as the original school. Uniquely composed of rock, the school still stands on the Howard W. Schott property on Highway 16 at San Geronimo. Fred Wendt attended the stone school for first and second grades.

Today Hank Schott and his wife, Beth (owners of the former schoolhouse), and their two daughters, Brookell and McKayla, live in the rock school.

Betty Lou Schott shared about her experience at Clifton in the 1940s: "I was in fifth grade when the school closed and then I went to Helotes. But I do remember we learned to square dance and we had a Victrola for music. The teacher even came to my house and we practiced dancing. My cousin Peggy Schott was four years older. It was my grandfather (August Schott) who donated the land."

A 1935 class photo for Clifton School
COURTESY MADELYN AND GARY SCHOTT

A 1947 class photo. Top Row: Betty Lou Schott, Walker G., Benny Martinez. Second Row: First four children unknown. Leora Schott, unknown, Kay Guerra, Yvonne Haby.
COURTESY MADELYN AND GARY SCHOTT

Leora Schott and an unidentified child pose at the Clifton School water pump in 1947.
COURTESY MADELYN AND GARY SCHOTT

According to the minutes of a Clifton School Board meeting: "[As of] December 11, 1950, Mr. Galm made the motion that the property known as the Clifton School property be sold to Mr. Howard Schott for the sum of ($1,000) one thousand dollars—with Mr. Schott bearing all expense on Title and Transfer. Dr. Burke seconded the motion. Motion carried."

According to Texas author Cindy (Irene) Sandell, "My father's mother, Paradine Durham, attended a small school called the Cottonwood School. Settlers first came to the area about 1870, I think, and organized the school as soon as they could. They called their little community Cottonwood Hole because of a fresh water spring nearby. (The Brazos River there is too salty for humans or animals to drink, so a fresh spring was important)."

Cottonwood School was a small one-room school.
COURTESY CINDY SANDELL

In the photo, taken in 1896, Cindy Sandell's grandmother Paradine is in the second row, fourth from the left.

COURTESY CINDY SANDELL

Cindy also recalled her father telling her a humorous, though revealing, story: "In those first days the school board hired a young woman to serve as the teacher. Anyone who wanted to learn to read could attend the school, so there was no age limit. When some wild cowboys from the Wichita Breaks showed up (who were way too old to be interested in learning), the result was fighting, bullying, and general disruption. Not able to control the chaos, the young woman quit. The community then hired a man. On his first day he showed up fully armed and lay a loaded revolver on the podium before starting class."

Chuckling, Cindy added, "Things calmed down quickly and the 'toughs,' as Dad called them, quickly disappeared. School commenced without a hitch."

Although the settlement of Waneta, Texas, can be traced back to 1835, the first school came much later; it was called the Red Prairie School and was located on land donated by Augustus Peterson, who had emigrated from Sweden. The school's first teachers were Mae Rae and Lola Dennis. A few years later the school was moved to William Lively's place. In 1913, Charles W. Butler, who had purchased land in 1852, donated a parcel and the school was moved again.

Red Prairie School and New Hope School were then combined and renamed the Waneta School. The new school opened in 1914, and to accommodate the school population, a third teacher was added. The oak frame schoolhouse with two chimneys served the Waneta Community until 1949, when it closed. Students were then incorporated into the Grapeland School District.

Wooster Common School No. 38 is believed to be the oldest existing one-room frame schoolhouse in Harris County, Texas. Built in 1894 on Scott's Bay, it was designed by Quincy A. Wooster on land donated by Junius Brown. Both Mr. Wooster and Mr. Brown had children that were being taught at home by Bertha Brown, Mr. Brown's daughter. The schoolhouse was built of cypress, and inside the school was a slate blackboard and new desks that had been purchased and delivered to the community by steamboat.

The schoolhouse was also an important community center and meetinghouse. Common School No. 38 became part of the Goose Creek Independent School District in 1919. It was closed and reopened several times, and then in 1980 it was relocated to the Republic of Texas Plaza in 1986, where it was restored. Finally, in 2006 the Wooster Schoolhouse was made a part of a living history museum complex.

UTAH

Federally mandated and publicly supported territorial schools emerged with the passage of Utah's first Free Public School Act by the Territorial Legislature in 1890. However, between 1867 and 1900, Congregational, Presbyterian, and Methodist mission boards established approximately one hundred private elementary and secondary schools, but these gave way as Utah's free public system took precedence.

Webster School in Mill Ward (Maeser, Utah) was built where the old Mud Temple was located before it burned. In this photo, taken circa 1895, teacher Robert Lewis Woodward is on the far right.
COURTESY VONITA BISHOP

Public secondary education did not exist in Utah until the 1890s, but by 1910, 58 percent of the state's sixteen- and seventeen-year-olds were enrolled in high school. In addition, beginning in the 1850s and 1860s, many of Utah's grammar schools were organized into wards where the Mormon church meetinghouse also served as the schoolhouse during the week. As the transcontinental railroad made Utah more accessible in 1869, many of the ward schools began to evolve into district public schools.

Robert Lewis Woodward (more often known as RL or Lew) was an enterprising young man who served as an early pioneer teacher in Ashley Valley from 1889 to 1903. According to his great-great-granddaughter, Vonita Hicks Bishop, Robert was born in Fountain Green, Sanpete County, in 1870. He was the youngest of twenty-eight children born to

Robert Lewis Woodward, here at age sixteen, grew up in Huntington, Emery County, and there learned to played cornet.
COURTESY VONITA BISHOP

his parents. "They each had children by other husbands and wives, and he had only one actual full brother, Don Carlos Woodward (who also grew up to become a teacher)."

When he was sixteen, RL received his teaching certificate, allowing him to teach grade school in Huntington. According to his journal (which he kept religiously throughout his life), he taught thirty students for the term. At seventeen, RL attended Brigham Young Academy in Provo, after which he returned to his teaching position. At eighteen he again returned to the Academy, but after typhoid fever hit Huntington, he returned home to help care for his family. He also fell ill, but after recovering returned to teaching.

RL applied to the Vernal School in Uintah County, but didn't get a teaching job until January 1889 in Maeser. The log cabin was called the "Mud Temple." RL taught all grades. Always a musician, he brought his cornet to Vernal, and then sold it to buy a bass viola. The local band often traveled all over to perform.

He wrote about his arrival, "I commenced my journey to Vernal the first of January, 1889, and arrived on the 3rd, there being a wedding going on when I got there. It was very cold coming, being 40 degrees below zero at Fort Duchesne when I stayed there."

RL also described his first week of school, after being warned by one of the school's trustees that some big boys would be hard to control. He wrote,

Wednesday was the day to look for trouble. When the noon hour was over I walked from my desk the 60 feet (length of the schoolroom), rang the bell but did not go back to replace the bell on the desk as I had done before. Instead I walked over to a window and listened. The big boys had gathered outside the building and didn't know I was listening to the plan they had to run me out. I watched them file in as planned. Joe's toe missed the bucket. As he took hold of it to tip the water out I grabbed him by the seat of his pants, shook him, stood him on his feet. Out of my pocket came the black "gutta-percha" [a type of plastic] ruler and I laid it on his palm a few times. He squawked good.

The other boys stood back. They hadn't moved. I said, "Now boys, if you care for some of the same I will oblige you. I came to teach this school and you or no one like you are going to stop me." Levi Bodily spoke up then, "I am with you." They all filed into their seats and that was the first and last of my trouble.

RL was also progressive. He wrote in the early 1890s, "I had made up my mind that our young folks needed a dance hall so they wouldn't have to go to Vernal which now supported two dance halls. . . . I got up to speak to an audience called after a Sunday evening meeting. I told them that we wanted 30 teams and wagons and two men with each team to go to the mountains and cut and haul logs into Dan Allen's mill. Dan had promised to saw the logs for our building. . . . I told them further that the flooring would be furnished us by some good brethren who were also interested in our young folks. . . . In no time at all we had our hall—a good size one too."

Apparently, Butch Cassidy—known to hide out nearby—liked to come into town when he was in the area to attend the dances. Reportedly the townsfolk liked him and he was always a perfect gentleman.

The hall was used for social gatherings as well as the church, and as a temporary school in Mill Ward while the brick schools of Bingham and Webster schools were built. It was used from 1890 until 1929.

RL married Annie Rosetta Searle in April 1889. Because he was nineteen and Annie was seventeen, they had to get their parents' permission. Each summer, he attended the Academy to improve his teaching. One time he rode his bike to get to Provo; it took five days.

Regarding RL's teaching, Phoebe C. Litster, a former student, wrote in 1949,

The best teacher we ever had was R.L. Woodward. We all feared him and we all loved and respected him. . . . There came a time when the trustees and parents got together and with "R.L's" help purchased modern furniture. How proud we were of those shining new desks; the little inkwells in the top were a wonder; the seats we could walk into and sit in comfort, a place to lean our backs. The teacher's desk was wonderful too. On it was a globe with the whole world mapped out on it. With his long pointer, Mr. Woodward showed us the different countries as they lay on the globe's surface. . . . Many were the

Taking a bus to Salt Lake City from Vernal, Utah. Robert, Maude and Rosetta are in the middle row.
COURTESY VONITA BISHOP

lessons we were taught and to this day R.L. Woodward calls us all his "boys and girls." . . . Well do we remember the black gutta-percha ruler, how it hurt when laid on our palms as the teacher held us by the finger.

The end of the log school was a sad loss to all. A fire destroyed the old schoolhouse in March 1892. The next schoolhouse was built of brick.

After teaching, RL went on to become a principal in Beaver, Utah, at the Murdock Academy, and his last formal job was in Millard County in the Deseret School District. There he was able to get the towns of Deseret and Oasis to consolidate and then to build the A. C. Nelson Elementary School between the two communities. Later he traveled all over the western states, including Montana, Idaho, Nebraska, Wyoming, Colorado, and Arizona. He delivered schoolbooks to outlying areas and schools.

🔔

Grafton, Utah, is now a ghost town, located just south of Zion National Park in Washington County. It is, however, one of Utah's most photographed towns and has been featured in several movies, including *Butch Cassidy and the Sundance Kid.*

Grafton was first settled in December 1859 as part of Brigham Young's plan to colonize southern Utah and establish cotton-growing farms.

The town grew quickly, and just as quickly outgrew the little log schoolhouse built in 1862. By 1864, an estimated twenty-eight families had settled there, and each farmed about an acre of land. Grafton became the county seat of Kane County for one year (1866–1867), and then changes to the county's borders in 1882 placed it inside Washington County.

Though the landscape is beautiful, the area is prone to flooding, and in 1862, flooding destroyed most of Grafton. One resident wrote, "The houses in old Grafton came floating down with the furniture, clothing and other property of the inhabitants, some of which was hauled out of the water, including three barrels of molasses." Grafton was relocated to a higher location about a mile upstream.

The community's farmers also had to dredge irrigation ditches frequently to clean out the silt from the river.

Still the pioneers persisted, and in 1886, Grafton's residents hauled lumber seventy-five miles from Mount Trumbull and gathered clay from a pit west of town to construct the adobe schoolhouse, which still stands. But when the local ward of the Church of Jesus Christ of Latter-day Saints was discontinued in 1921, the town's demise was imminent. Grafton's remaining residents left the town in 1944.

The town's plight was recognized in 1997, when the Grafton Heritage Partnership was organized to protect, preserve, and restore the community. With cooperation from former residents, the Utah State Historical Society, the Bureau of Land Management, the Utah Division of State History, and others, the old church and schoolhouse were restored.

🔔

The Torrey Log Church–Schoolhouse was built in Torrey, Wayne County, Utah, in 1898 as a Church of Jesus Christ of Latter-day Saints school and meetinghouse. The one-story log structure served as the school until 1917. The log building was constructed with sawn logs joined at the corners with half-dovetail notching. The logs were originally chinked with white mortar. The structure boasted a Greek revival influence, unusual for frontier schools, while the school's shingled hip roof flared up at the eaves. There was a bell tower over the front door.

The Torrey Schoolhouse continued to be used as a meeting place for the local Daughters of Utah Pioneers chapter until the 1970s. The school was nominated for inclusion on the National Register of Historic Places in 1993. It has since been fully restored.

In Junction, Utah, education was a priority. Classes were conducted for two years outside before the Fruita School could be built. Even though only eight families lived in Junction, these farmers had large families. The Behunins had thirteen children, and young Nettie, one of them, became the first schoolteacher when she was only twelve or thirteen. Her first class had twenty-two students, three of whom were her siblings, and she taught in her parents' backyard. She continued to teach outside until 1896 when the school building was completed. Elijah Cutler Behunin donated the land for the Fruita School.

Originally, the school had a flat, dirt-covered roof. A peaked, shingled roof was added in 1912 or 1913. The interior walls were built of chinked logs but later plastered. The desks were homemade, constructed of pine, with seats for two students each. Reportedly, teachers often sat an unruly boy alongside a girl, which was considered a humiliating act.

In 1900, the Fruita schoolhouse was loaned to the Wayne County School District for its first county-approved classes. Nettie Behunin, then twenty-two, was the teacher. She received $70 a month even though male teachers were paid $80 per month. The school was eventually closed in 1941. In 1964, the National Park Service nominated the school to be listed in the National Register of Historic Places.

WASHINGTON

It's been documented that schools have existed in the state of Washington since the 1830s, although there is some discrepancy as to which of two men first introduced formal education. Many believe that in 1830, near Spokane, Washington, Spokan Garry, a Native American from a local tribe, returned from a Canadian boarding school and began to teach his people. The schoolhouse was little more than a pole structure, covered over with tule (bunch grass) reed mats. Supposedly he taught from the Bible and other materials he'd been given during his five years at an Episcopalian school.

Others believe that a Yankee schoolmaster named John Ball became the first teacher in Washington when he conducted classes for children at Fort Vancouver in 1832.

In 1836, missionaries Marcus Whitman and H. H. Spalding established a school for Indian children in Walla Walla, Washington Territory.

In 1852, the first real public school opened in Olympia, Washington. This was one year before the new territory of Washington became separate from Oregon Territory.

The first school in Spokane, Washington, was built circa 1878 and was used until 1883. The school was then briefly occupied by Spokane's first newspaper, the *Spokane Falls Review*. In 1889, the small frame school burned in Spokane's Great Fire of 1889.

With the end of the Civil War and the completion of the transcontinental railroad, Washington Territory grew quickly; likewise the number of one-room schools grew. In 1869, there were twenty-two one-room schools; in 1872, the territorial school superintendent reported there were 222 districts, 157 schools, 144 schoolhouses, and almost 4,000 students in the Territory.

Winton Elementary, a one-room school east of Seattle, was built in 1915. The school on Shaw Island, Washington, was built in 1890 and is listed in the National Register of Historic Places.

Interestingly, the first separate teacherage was built in Walla Walla County, Washington, in 1905. The idea—which originated in northern European countries—was soon adopted by many schools throughout the West. Before this time, of course, teachers boarded with families. By 1921, there were forty-three teacherages in South Dakota alone. By the time Washington was admitted to the Union, in 1889, there were one thousand schools across the state.

By the end of the nineteenth century, old log schools were being replaced by modestly sized wood structures, and by the turn of the century, most of the 2,888 schools in Washington were framed in wood. However, in 1908, school districts began demanding that schools be built of stone or brick as protection against fire. In addition, many began to install indoor plumbing.

🔔

Pleasant Valley School was built on Orcas Island, in San Juan County, in 1888, before Washington was a state. At various times the one-room school, which was renamed the Crow Valley School, had up to forty-seven students. The school closed in 1918, but it wasn't until 1987 that it was put on the National Register of Historic Places. Then in 2011, it was deeded by its owners, Richard Schneider and Bud McBride, to the Orcas Island Historical Museum.

🔔

Diane Biggar Taylor attended a one-room school near Colville, Washington. Colville is home to the Keller Heritage Center, which features the Stevens County Historical

Society Museum, the Keller House, a machinery museum, Colville's first schoolhouse, a homestead cabin, and a Forest Service fire lookout.

About her school years, Diane wrote, "We had a good teacher and a varied program. We had a different kind of music every morning (i.e.: band, singing, square dancing, marching, etc).

"I still remember how embarrassed I was in the third grade when I spoke up to answer a geography question that the teacher had asked of the 7th and 8th grade classes. I answered before anyone else; it just popped out of my mouth. In those days, you didn't speak up unless spoken to! I guess it goes to show that I was learning not only my own work but things that the older kids were learning, too. (I had a strange feeling that the teacher was rather proud of me for knowing the answer, although she never mentioned the incident)."

Washington's Oysterville School, built in 1908, shown here circa 1950s
COURTESY GAIL L. JENNER COLLECTION

Diane continued, "At recess, we worked on building a log house; the older boys cut down the trees. We probably had the walls up four feet before I had to move from that school. We also played drop the handkerchief, 'ante over', flying Dutchman, hide and seek, and other similar old-fashioned games. In the winter, we spent the recess sledding or sliding."

Diane summarized her experience by adding, "Those were the good old days, even though we had to walk two and a half miles each way. Lots of times my younger sister and I would ride our horse, Jerry, to school and then send him home. (He refused to take us to school in the winter when it was icy). But I can't remember ever not wanting to go to school!"

🔔

Betty Trueax McClelland attended a one-room school in first grade. She walked a mile and a half to school. She recalled, "Because we lived at the end of a gravel road, with forest between our home and the other homes, my mom would walk down and wait for me there with my little brother." As to her experiences attending the small rural school, she noted, "The teacher there let me read ahead, which is why when I moved to a larger school in second grade, I had to reread the books I'd already read."

Later, when she and her husband moved out to their farm, her kids attended a country school for grades one through six, "with two teachers, a library, and a room for the holiday events. The school had a basement where spaghetti feeds were held to raise money. . . . I am grateful my kids had that experience."

🔔

Prairie View School, in Waverly, Spokane County, Washington, was a little one-room schoolhouse that opened in 1904 and closed in 1936. It was one of at least 130 one-room schools located in Spokane County in the late 1920s, and there were perhaps just as many in Whitman County.

The Prairie View schoolhouse was built for grades K–12, but it was not the town's first school. In 1881, the first school was a simple log cabin. A few years later the town constructed the Prairie View schoolhouse.

Annie Holtman served as its teacher from 1923 until 1961. According to historian Glenn Leitz, before the school closed its doors in 1937, there were as many as thirty to forty students at Prairie View each year. Thankfully, in 2013, the Southeast Spokane County Historical Society moved the building from its original foundation to its current location.

Normal School

On October 13, 1890, teacher education was enhanced when the State Normal School at Cheney was opened. Sixteen students enrolled, each of them meeting the following criteria: The student must be 1) at least sixteen years old, 2) of good moral character, 3) in good health, 4) recommended by a county school superintendent, and 5) able to pass a basic exam of subjects to be covered in grammar school.

The State Normal School was a college for training teachers. The name "Normal School" came from the French "ecole normale." Three State Normal Schools opened up after Washington achieved statehood in 1889.

"At this time, nearly every city, town and village in the state was clamoring for a state institution," wrote former mayor D. F. Percival in the *Cheney Free Press* (Oliphant). While the cities of Bellingham and Ellensburg were also granted schools, Cheney had a school building and was ready to start. The location had been part of the Benjamin P. Cheney Academy, which was supported by the Northern Pacific Railroad director in 1881.

By the end of the first year, enrollment at Cheney jumped to fifty. The school eventually became the Eastern Washington College of Education in 1937; it was renamed Eastern Washington State College in 1961, and lastly named Eastern Washington University in 1977.

Cheney Normal School eventually became Eastern Washington College of Education, then Eastern Washington State College, and finally Eastern Washington University.
COURTESY GAIL L. JENNER COLLECTION

WYOMING

A thousand pioneer schools once dotted the Wyoming landscape. Reportedly, the first recorded school in Wyoming was established for officers' and traders' children at Fort Laramie in 1852. In 1860, Judge W. A. Carter founded a second school at Fort Bridger.

The first public school, while supported by subscription, was open to all students. It was established in 1868 in Cheyenne, Wyoming. In 1869, two more subscription-supported public schools were opened in Laramie and Rawlins. By 1870, there were four public schools and five day and boarding schools in the Territory, including a subscription public school in Evanston and a private school at South Pass.

In 1871, the first school for Native American school children was created by the Episcopal Church and housed in an old log building at Fort Washakie on the Wind River Reservation. In 1873, the Wyoming territorial government instituted compulsory education for all students, ages seven through sixteen. At this time there were eight public schools and three private schools.

The school at Fort Bridger was established in 1860.
COURTESY GAIL L. JENNER COLLECTION

This chapel was built for the Shoshone Episcopal Mission by the Reverend John Roberts. It was originally used both for religious services and as a classroom for the Mission Boarding School.
COURTESY LIBRARY OF CONGRESS

In 1878, the East Side School was established in Laramie; today the two-story brick East
Side School is the oldest public school in Wyoming. In 1879, a school was established at
Fort Washakie. Reportedly, there were forty-nine teachers in twenty-five schools teaching
a total of 2,090 students within the territory.

It wasn't until 1884 that an adobe schoolhouse was built for Shoshone and Arapaho students southwest of Fort Washakie on the Wind River Reservation. And in 1888, Sisters
of Charity from Leavenworth, Kansas started a boarding school in their convent at St.
Stephens on the reservation. The Catholic Church ran the school until 1975.

The Lower Shell School was built in 1903 in the Big Horn Valley. It was one of the first structures not to be built of logs. The school functioned as a church and Sunday school, and as a meeting hall. It was used as a school until the 1950s, and as a community hall until the 1970s.
CAROL M. HIGHSMITH PHOTOGRAPHER/COURTESY LIBRARY OF CONGRESS

Meeteetse, translated as "meeting place" in Shoshone, is one of the oldest settlements in the Big Horn Basin and dates back to the late 1870s; the town's post office and schoolhouse date to 1880. In 1881, Meeteetse became a stop on the old Meeteetse Trail, which the army built as a stage and freight road from Red Lodge, Montana.

In the 1890s, Meeteetse became the jumping off place for a minor gold rush to the upper Wood Valley, where, in 1885, William Kirwin discovered gold.

A number of mines were developed, including the Molly Logan, the Smuggler, and the Tumlum. The Tumlum was the deepest mine in the area, at 250 feet deep, and gold was brought up and out by mule.

The gold and silver mining town of Kirwin, Wyoming, located outside of Meeteetse, was founded high on the Wood River in 1885. By 1894, the Shoshone River Mining

The Ayers School, in Wheatland, Wyoming, was constructed circa 1904.
COURTESY GAIL L. JENNER COLLECTION

Company was formed and the company's ore was being shipped from Kirwin by mule in 1897. Kirwin became a well-established community, with two hundred people and thirty-eight buildings, including boarding houses, a hotel, a sawmill, a post office, stores, and houses—but no cemetery, saloons, or brothels.

In February 1907, several severe blizzards swept through Kirwin, including one that dumped fifty feet of snow. On the heels of that, an avalanche—referred to as the "White Death" of the Rockies—roared down onto Charles L. Tewksbury's Store. Three patrons were killed. The town's spirit was broken and everyone but Charles Tewksbury abandoned Kirwin.

🔔

In 1903, the Lower Shell School was built in Big Horn County, Wyoming. It was one of the first structures in the area to not use log construction. It was used as a school into the 1950s and as a community hall until the 1970s. In 1985, it was listed on the National Register of Historic Places.

By 1905, there were a total of 18,902 students in Wyoming, attending 716 schools, taught by 797 teachers. In 1934, Wyoming reported a total of 385 school districts across the state, including 1,033 rural schools (with 934 one-room schools). In 1935, the WPA funded construction of twenty-one new schools and ninety-two school reconstruction projects. In addition, the Wyoming legislature established the first funding to equalize spending for poorer schools in the state.

Epilogue

WHILE THERE WAS AND IS NO WAY TO CATALOGUE ALL THE ONE-ROOM SCHOOLS THAT ever existed across the pioneer West, the journey to locate the individuals who were shaped by them and the unique schools that once dotted the landscape—and still do in some cases—was an intensely satisfying one. People from all over wrote to me to share their families' or their personal stories and fond recollections of the teachers and schools where they were educated.

The final chapter of this volume, however, cannot be written. Part of this is due to the fact that in some places, the one-room school is not yet fading into memory. In places like Montana, the Dakotas, Wyoming, and Alaska, they are still a part of the educational fabric of the state, and in many places, schools are open to serve only a handful of students. However, as former one-room school teacher Lester Newton explained, "The size of a school is/was determined by the days a student was actually present in school. If attendance for the school year averaged less than six, the school would lapse. . . . It took at least seven or eight students to stay above the magic number of six."

In spite of the extra workload facing the teacher in the one-room school, especially these days, the satisfaction of teachers with their jobs seems to be very high. According to Dawn Shlaudeman, who taught at two different one-room schools in Montana, "Those were the best teaching years I ever had."

Shlaudeman shared that she "taught in Sand Springs, Montana, from 1997 to 1998. It was my very first job. I had ten students from three different families. I taught K-8 and had three girls and seven boys. The only thing in Sand Springs was the school, a tiny store/post office, a church, and a farmhouse in the distance." And even near the end of the twentieth century, the amenities at the school—where Shlaudeman also lived—were few. As she explained:

EPILOGUE

The Sand Springs teacherage was very cold and basic. It had lots of mice. I remember cooking one night and a little ball of flame came running out from under the oven! I don't know where that mouse was inside there, but he found his way out. I also remember another time when I was teaching, a paper lunch bag went scurrying across the floor.

I should add that the water was not drinkable. I took showers in rusty water and had to take my whites somewhere else to wash, to the town of Jordan or to my parents' house an hour and a half away. To get drinking water I had to drive to Jordan sixty miles away.

Speaking of lunches, the mothers would take turns making us the best home-cooked meals on Fridays. A lot of the moms and a few dads would join us. I also had many

This is a newer photo of the school in Sand Springs, Montana. According to Heidi Thomas, "In recent years, the schoolhouse was moved across the highway to where a new store was built, and a small two-room building was constructed to be used by the teacher."
COURTESY SANDY GIBSON

meals with the different families and once in a while I would go horseback riding in the evenings with some of the kids. The families made me feel so welcome.

There were about ten other one-room schools in session that year. The teachers would try to get together once a month to exchange ideas. The school closest to me, Big Dry, would join us for Halloween parties, Easter parties, field/track days, and together we put on an outstanding musical Christmas program (a play called "Holly and the Ivy League").

I loved that job! You were so busy you had no time to get lonely. I had nine grade levels to prepare for with eight subjects each. I also had to teach P.E. and music as well as be the janitor, the secretary, and the principal. It was a great way to start my career. I learned early on how important it is to be organized.

Shlaudeman would go on to teach at the one-room Nye, Montana, school from 1998 to 2002, where she had at most seventeen students. (In 2018, the school served four children.) The classroom was the upper room of a two-story river-rock school building constructed at the base of the Beartooth Mountains. In that small community on the Stillwater River, made up of farmers', ranchers' and miners' families, she was again the teacher, the secretary, the principal, and the P.E. teacher, but a local music teacher came in once a week—and there was a janitor.

Dawn Shlaudeman's story is just one from the so many worthy and deserving stories of rural schoolhouses and structures—and it represents those stories that have not been told or those stories that are vanishing quickly. To lose this history, however, is an American tragedy. The thousands of individuals—from every walk of life—who passed through the gates and entryways into these schools carry the impact of their small school experiences (good and bad) deep within their souls.

It became quite clear to me in the process of researching one-room schools that the commonality of being a part of such a school was more about character-building and human relationship than about curriculum, or the famous "three Rs".

Preserving history is no small feat and it makes no small contribution to the total compilation of the American experience. Thankfully, efforts are being made in many locations, on an individual, community, state, and federal level, to capture these experiences. I can only express my hope that more stories and photographs, names and locations can be gathered up by those living in proximity to them. Before the last walls and square nails or mortar falls to the ground, or before the last teacher of vintage schools passes on, it would be a noble enterprise for local historians to go out and collect these fascinating and unique histories.

Bibliography

"A Guide for Research." *Country School Journal*, Country School Association of America, www.country schooljournal.com/A_GUIDE_FOR_RESARCH.html. Accessed May 7, 2017.

"About the Homestead Act." National Park Service, www.nps.gov/home/learn/historyculture/abouthome steadactlaw.htm. Accessed June 10, 2017.

Alvord, Sam, personal narrative, November 15, 2017.

"American Revolution: 1776 Nathan Hale Volunteers to Spy Behind British Lines." History Channel, www .history.com/this-day-in-history/nathan-hale-volunteers-to-spy-behind-british-lines. Accessed July 2, 2017.

"America's One Rooms." One-room Schoolhouse Center, http://oneroomschoolhousecenter.weebly.com/ americas-one-rooms.html. Accessed May 8, 2017.

"Anchorage 1910–1940, Legends & Legacies." Alaskahistory.org, www.alaskahistory.org/anchorage-time line/. Accessed February 20, 2018.

"Area History." Arnold, the Heart of the Sierra, cometoarnold.com/visitors-guide/area-history/.

Arrington, Todd. "Abraham Lincoln and the West." National Park Service, www.nps.gov/home/learn/his toryculture/lincolnandwest.htm. Accessed July 13, 2017.

"Ballston, Oregon." Revolvy, www.revolvy.com/main/index.php?s=Ballston,%20Oregon. Accessed May 21, 2017.

Bandy, Paula. "Ruch School Turns 100." *Southern Oregon Magazine*, March 23, 2014, www.southernoregon magazine.com/ruch-school.

Baytown Historical Preservation Association, Baytownhistory.org, http://baytownhistory.org/home.html. Accessed September 3, 2017.

Bishop, Bruce, personal narrative, December 13, 2017.

Bishop, Vonita, personal narrative, December 14, 2017.

Blair, Edward. *Leadville: Colorado's Magic City*. Boulder, CO: Pruett Publishing Company, 1980.

"Booker T. Washington (1856–1915)." *Encyclopedia of Southern Culture*, eds. Charles Reagan Wilson and William Ferris, Chapel Hill: University of North Carolina Press, 1989, http://docsouth.unc.edu/fpn/ washington/bio.html.

Bushy, Judy. "Our Happy Camp Log High School Built 1933." HappyCampHistory.com, January 21, 2011, http://happycamphistory.com/our-happy-camp-log-high-school-built-1933/.

Caldwell, Charlotte. *Visions and Voices: Montana's One-Room Schoolhouses*. Clyde Park, MT: Barn Board Press, 2012.

"Calico Ghost Town, California." Ghosttownexplorers.org, www.ghosttownexplorers.org/california/calico/ calico.htm. Accessed October 19, 2017.

BIBLIOGRAPHY

Campbell, John Martin. *The Prairie Schoolhouse*. Albuquerque: University of New Mexico Press, 1996.

"Children's Lives at the Turn of the Twentieth Century." Teacher's Guide Primary Source Set. Library of Congress Teaching with Primary Sources, loc.gov/teachers.

Christopher, Jeri, personal narrative, June 5, 2017.

Clegg, Luther Bryan. *The Empty Schoolhouse: Memories of One-Room Texas Schools*. College Station: Texas A&M University Press, 1997.

Colby, Merle. *A Guide to Alaska: Last American Frontier*. New York: The Macmillan Company, 1943.

"Posts from June 2010." Country School Association of America, http://csaa.typepad.com/country_school_association/2010/06/index.html.

"Crown King's One-Room School Celebrates Century of One-on-One Teaching." *Prescott Woman*, August/September 2017, pp. 52–53, http://online.fliphtml5.com/ebse/icdg/#p=54.

"Digital Horizons: Life on the Northern Plains." State Historical Society of North Dakota, www.digitalhorizonsonline.org/digital/collection/uw-ndshs/id/8511/rec/13. Accessed July 18, 2017.

Easley, Cheryl. *Boarding School: Historical Trauma among Alaska's Native People*. Anchorage: The National Resource Center for American Indian, Alaska Native and Native Hawaiian Elders, University of Alaska, 2006.

"Elaine Goodale Eastman (1863–1953)." Only a Teacher: Schoolhouse Pioneers, PBS, www.pbs.org/onlyateacher/elaine.html. Accessed August 22, 2017.

"Esperanza's World—Early Tucson Center—Schools." Arizona Historical Society, www.arizonahistoricalsociety.org/education/esperanza/tucson/schools/. Accessed July 14, 2017.

"Fargo, North Dakota: Its History and Images." NDSU Archives, https://library.ndsu.edu/fargo-history/?q=content/public-schools. Accessed July 15, 2017.

Farrington, Sharon, personal interview, January 20, 2018.

Frazier, Joseph B. "One-Room Schools Still Part of Life in Eastern Oregon." *Seattle Times*, November 15, 1998.

French, Eugene M. *Reminiscences of the Past: Siskiyou County*, ed. Nancy French Zurflueh, 1992.

"Grizzly Bluff School." Wow.com, www.wow.com/wiki/Grizzly_Bluff_School. Accessed August 6, 2017.

Gulliford, Andrew. *America's Country Schools*. Washington: The Preservation Press, 1984.

Head, Vic. "One-Room Schoolhouse." Alpine Historical Society, www.alpinehistory.org/one_room_schoolhouse.html. Accessed August 11, 2017.

"Historic Schools of Wyoming." Wyoming SHPO, http://wyoshpo.state.wy.us/Schools/Index.aspx. Accessed September 16, 2017.

History of Humboldt County California, with Illustrations. San Francisco: Wallace W. Elliott & Co., Publishers, 1882.

"History of Medford, The." Medford Oregon History, www.ci.medford.or.us/Page.asp?NavID=2990. Accessed September 21, 2017.

Hoffman, Nancy. *Woman's "True" Profession: Voices from the History of Teaching*, Cambridge, MA: Harvard Education Press, 2003.

"Homestead Act of 1862, The." National Park Service, www.nps.gov/home/learn/historyculture/upload/MW,pdf,Homestead%20Act,txt.pdf. Accessed May 29, 2017.

Iannios, Demetrios, personal narrative. March 1, 2018.

In Picture-Land: Blue Bell Series. New York: McLoughlin Brothers, 1896.

"Intermountain Indian School." Wikipedia, https://en.wikipedia.org/wiki/Intermountain_Indian_School. Accessed August 26, 2017.

Jenner, GloryAnn, personal narrative, September 8, 2017.

BIBLIOGRAPHY

"Junction School." National Park Service, March 31, 2012, www.nps.gov/lyjo/planyourvisit/junctionschool .htm. Accessed September 18, 2017.

"Land Grant College Act of 1862." *Encyclopaedia Britannica*, www.britannica.com/topic/Land-Grant-Col lege-Act-of-1862. Accessed May 8, 2017.

Lansford, Lynn Milburn. *Milburn: The Birth of a Pioneer Town and the Love Story That Began There*. CreateSpace Independent Publishing Platform, 2015.

Maplesden, Carol, personal narrative, September 15, 2017.

Maplesden, Larry, personal narrative, November 8, 2017.

Massey, Cynthia Leal, personal narrative, October 23, 2017.

Massey, Cynthia Leal. *Helotes: Where the Texas Hill Country Begins*. Talequah, OK: Old American Publishing, 2008.

"McClanahans, The." Goodsprings Historical Society, www.goodsprings.org/mcclan.php. Accessed September 1, 2017.

Moberg, Lisa. "The One-Room School." Stories from School AZ, November 21, 2014, www.storiesfrom schoolaz.org/one-room-school/. Accessed September 1, 2017.

"Mount Trumbull." Ghosttowns.com, http://ghosttowns.com/states/az/mounttrumbull.html. Accessed July 18, 2017.

Munn, Vella, personal narrative, July 10, 2017.

Murnin, Chrissie. "Couple Get 'Schooled' on Historic Home." *San Antonio Express-News*, July 15, 2012.

"New England Primer—1860." Virtue, Liberty and Independence, December 6, 2011. http://liberty-virtue -independence.blogspot.com/2011/12/new-england-primer-1691.html.

Newcomb, Lois Kennedy, personal narrative, May 23, 2017.

"NISD Roots Go Back More Than a Century." Northside ISD, November 4, 2011, https://nisd.net/news/ articles/2153. Accessed September 6, 2017.

O'Neill, Mary. "The New England Primer." https://www3.nd.edu/~rbarger/www7/neprimer.html. Accessed May 30, 2017.

"One Room Schoolhouse, The." Scottsdale Historic Museum and Schoolhouse, www.scottsdalemuseum .com/index.php/exhibits/permanent/the-one-room-schoolhouse. Accessed July 20, 2017.

"Oregon Historic Sites Database." Oregon State Parks, http://heritagedata.prd.state.or.us/historic/index .cfm?do=v.dsp_siteSummary&resultDisplay=36142. Accessed August 11, 2017.

Pehrson, Nolan and Ruth Dungan. "Kenyon School Sketches." In *The Covered Wagon, 1994*, 32–37. Redding, CA: Shasta Historical Society,.

Pinehurst School Community. *Pinehurst School: 100 Years of Growing up on the Greensprings*. Pinehurst, OR: Pinehurst School Foundation, 2008.

Plain, Nancy, personal narrative, November 10, 2017.

Quigley, Harriett, personal narrative, November 3, 2017.

"Railroad Era: 1881 to 1912, The." Las Cruces: Crossroads of History, www.las-cruces.org/code/history_ exhibit/railroad.html. Accessed June 27, 2017.

Ramos, Mary G. "A Boost for Black Education in the Early 20th Century." Rosenwald Schools in Texas, Texas State Historical Association, http://texasalmanac.com/topics/history/rosenwald-schools-texas. Accessed July 22, 2017.

Rocheleau, Paul. *The One-Room Schoolhouse: A Tribute to a Beloved National Icon*. New York: Universe, 2003.

"Rosenwald Schools, The: Progressive Era Philanthropy in the Segregated South." National Park Service, www.nps.gov/nr/twhp/wwwlps/lessons/159rosenwald/159rosenwald.htm. Accessed September 8, 2017.

Sandahl, Shari Fiock, personal narrative, July 15, 2017.

BIBLIOGRAPHY

Sandall, Irene (Cindy), personal narrative, October 22, 2017.

"Schoolmarms." One Room Schoolhouse Center, http://oneroomschoolhousecenter.weebly.com/school marms.html. Accessed May 12, 2017.

Schoerner, Grace S. *Under One Roof: A Traveler's Guide to America's One-room Schoolhouse Museums*. Pine, AZ: Pine-Strawberry Archeological & Historical Society, 2000. Accessed June 27, 2017.

"Schoolhouse at Calico, California, The." Walkerhomeschoolblog, September 14, 2015, https://walkerhome schoolblog.wordpress.com/2015/09/14/the-schoolhouse-at-calico-california/.

Shockey, Christopher. "Pinehurst School History Dates Back to 1908." Jefferson Public Radio, February 27, 2014, http://ijpr.org/post/pinehurst-school-history-dates-back-1908#stream/0. Accessed May 12, 2017.

Schott, Betty Lou, personal narrative, November 12, 2017.

Spencer, Matthew. "Nebraska's One-Room Schoolhouses." *Nebraska Life Magazine,* September/October 2013, http://www.nebraskalife.com/Nebraskas-One-Room-Schoolhouses/. Accessed August 11, 2017.

Stephens, Donna M. *One-Room School: Teaching in the 1930s Western Oklahoma*. Norman: University of Oklahoma Press, 1990.

Stewart, Annette. "Old One-Two Room School Houses." *Arcanum Wayne Trail Historical Society, Inc.* 12, no. 4 (September 2016).

"Strawberry Schoolhouse." Pine-Strawberry Archeological and Historical Society, www.pinestrawhs.org/ schoolhouse.html. Accessed July 13, 2017.

Takores, Lauren. "Two-Room Schoolhouse Serves Grades K-5 in Damman." *Daily Record*, June 13, 2014, www.dailyrecordnews.com/members/two-room-schoolhouse-serves-grades-k-in-dammon-article_ 81df4d82-f323-11e3-8f9f-001a4bcf887a.html.

Texas Public Schools Sesquicentennial Handbook 1854–2004. Texas Education Agency. https://tea.texas.gov/ About_TEA/Welcome_and_Overview/. Accessed June 13, 2017.

Texas Schoolhouse (Prior to 1950), The." TexasEscapes.com, www.texasescapes.com/Texas_architecture/ TexasSchoolhouses/TexasSchoolhouses.htm. June 17, 2017.

"Timeline of Wyoming School History." Wyoming SHPO, http://wyoshpo.state.wy.us/Schools/History/ Timeline.aspx. Accessed July 6, 2017.

Trinity 1963–1965. Yearbook of the Trinity County Historical Society, Weaverville, CA.

Turner, Kernan. "Settlers Build School of Dove-Tailed Hand-Hewn Logs." Jefferson Public Radio, March 30, 2017, http://ijpr.org/post/settlers-build-school-dovetailed-handhewn-logs#stream/0.

"Unit 7: Set 4: Rural & Town Schools—Introduction." State Historical Society of North Dakota, http:// history.nd.gov/textbook/unit7_prettygood/unit7_4_intro.html. Accessed April 28, 2017.

"Walnut School." Rootsweb, www.rootsweb.ancestry.com/-txcoke/School/walnut_html. Accessed May 4, 2017.

Weis, Norman D. *Ghost Towns of the Northwest*. Caldwell, ID: Caxton Printers, Ltd., 1974.

Wells, Harry L. *History of Siskiyou County, California*. Oakland, CA: D. J. Stewart & Co., 1881.

Wheeling, Jennifer, personal narrative, October 23, 2017.

Wheeling, Joe, personal narrative, October 23, 2017.

White, Royce. "A Brief History of Butte Valley High School." May 24, 1963.

Wilson, Norma C. and Charles L. Woodard. *One-Room Country School: South Dakota Stories*. Brookings: South Dakota Humanities Foundation, 1998.

Woodward, Tim. "A Hundred Years at a One-Room School," *Seattle Times*, November 15, 2010.

Wright, Jan. "Talent." *The Oregon Encyclopedia*, https://oregonencyclopedia.org/articles/talent/#.WhMq1IX-rypo. Accessed July 20, 2017.

Zorbas, Elaine. *Fiddletown Schoolhouse Memories*. Fiddletown, CA: Fiddletown Preservation Society, Inc., 2012.

Index

Italicized page numbers indicate photographs.

A. C. Nelson Elementary School, Utah, 147
Aandahl, Fred George, 110
Acorn Academy, Colorado, 69–70
Adams, John, 2
adobe construction, 8, 52, 148
African Americans
  college admission, 122
  communities of, 81–82
  education of, 114
  schools for, 117, 128–29, *129*
  slavery, 32
Alaska
  education policies, 37, 39
  history of, 34, 38
  immigrant populations in, 35–36, *36*
  mining in, *35*, 38, 40
  native populations and education, 35, 36, 37, *38*, 38–40
  schoolhouses in, 36–39
  teacher salaries in, 38
Aleuts, 36
alphabet memorization, 6–7
Altaville Grammar School, California, 50, *50*, *51*
Alvord, Sam, 125
Americanization Act, 132
America's Country Schools (Gulliford), 85, 104
Anaheim, California, 52–53
Anchorage, Alaska, 36–37
Anderson, Carrie, 128
Apache, 41–42, 43
Apache Elementary School, Arizona, 42
Applegate Trail, 130

Arapaho, 155
arithmetic, 5, 15, 17, 83, 88, 116
Arizona
  history of, 40
  native populations and education, *42*, 42–43, 104
  schoolhouses in, 40–44, *43*, *44*
Ash Grove School, Oklahoma, 117
Athapascan Indians, 36
Atondo, Rose, 12
attendance, 2, 67, 132, 158
avalanches, 157
Averill, Maxine, 80

Bailey, George Washington Riley, 125
Ball, John, 149
Bannack Schoolhouse, Montana, 87, *87*, 89
Barclay School, Nevada, 103
barns
  as school horse stables, 56, 72, 93, *113*
  as temporary school locations, 139
Barnum, Rosalea, *60*
Barton, Chester, 17
Battle of Brazito, 108
Beadle, William Henry Harrison, 131
Beaver Creek School, Oregon, 127
Beekman, C. C., 127
behavior. *See* deportment
Behunin, Elijah Cutler, 149
Behunin, Nettie, 149
Bellgrove School, Idaho, 76
bells, 17, 62, 65, 72
bell towers, 52, 55, 103, 110, 124, 125, 148

benches, *1,* 121, 122
Benjamin P. Cheney Academy, 153
Bennett, Grace, 17
Bethel Mennonite Church, 131
BIA (Bureau of Indian Affairs), 39, 44, 108
Bibbens, Elsie, 25
Bible, 6–7, 149
Bishop, Barbara, 71–72
Bishop, Bruce, 71–72
Bishop, Vonita Hicks, 144
Bishop, W. R., 122
Bishop, Wilbur, 72
Bismarck, North Dakota, 110, *110*
blab schools, 5, 15
Black, Sarah, 42
blackboard erasers, 17
blackboards, 17, 108, 118, 136, 143. *See also* slates
blind students, 4
blizzards, 95, *96,* 134, 157
board-and-batten construction, 8, 71, 103
Boarding School: Historical Trauma among Alaska's Native People (Easley), 37
boarding schools
    in Alaskan, 37, 38–40
    in Arizona, *43,* 43–44, *44*
    cultural consequences of, 39, 131
    government policies on, 114
    in Kansas, 79
    in New Mexico, 107, *107,* 108
    opposition to, 114
    purpose, 37, 43, 44, 114
    in South Dakota, 131–32
    in Wyoming, 154, 155
Bogus Elementary, California, 12, *13*
Boley, Oklahoma, 81
bonds, 52–53, 125, 135
books
    classroom libraries for, 130
    crib, 5, 6
    Native American culture and, 132
    for reading lessons, 5, 7, *7,* 88
    textbooks, 117
box auctions, 134

boys
    education importance, 11
    fire-building responsibilities, 31
    industrial schools for, 37
    pranks by, 21, 27, 30
    teachers challenged by, 17
    wood-splitting chores of, 10
Brackett Creek School, Montana, 11
Brady, Josey, 95
Brandeis, Louis, 132
Brannan, Sam, 45
Brauchle, Henry T., 136
Braunsport, Oregon, 119
Brewick, Gladys, 134
brick construction, 78, 93–94, 115, 150
Brigham Young Academy, 145, 146
Broday, John G., 37
Brooklyn (ship), 44
Brown, Bertha, 143
Brown, Irene Bennett, 124
Brown, Junius, 143
Brown, Oda, 29
Brown, William, 128
Brown School, South Dakota, 131
Brown's School, Colorado, 70
Bryan, Leona Lewis, 21
Buchanan, James, 32
Buena Vista One-Room Schoolhouse, Nevada, 103
Bundyville, Arizona, 41
Burch, Mrs., 67
Bureau of Indian Affairs (BIA), 39, 44, 108
buses, 11, 59, 72, *147*
Butch Cassidy and the Sundance Kid (movie), 147
Butler, Charles W., 143
Butler, Dorothy Pitts, 58

Cadman, John, 93
California
    class photos of students, *3, 27, 50, 54, 57, 61, 67*
    classroom views, *68*
    class size minimums, 67
    colonial settlements in, 52
    courthouses in, *68*

dress codes, 58
education policies, 48–49, 57
exterior views, *22, 23*
gold rush history, 24, 32, 44, *45*
immigrant populations, 52, 57, *57,* 64
interracial marriages in, 47, *47*
missionary schools, 45
modern use of one-room schools in, 2, 61
population growth and statistics, 45, 47
reunions, *63*
schoolhouse, first, 45
schoolhouses in, *49,* 49–58, *51, 54, 56,* 59, *60, 61,* 61–65, *66, 69*
schoolhouses relocated to museums, 56, *66*
state fair field trips, 25
student experiences, 61–63
teacher institute workshops in, 26–27
teacher residences, 21
teaching experiences, 14–15, 23–24, 30
teaching supplies from, *17*
westward movement to, 44–47, *46*
wildlife encounters, 53
winter conditions, 10, 21–22
women in, *47,* 47–48, *48*
Callahan School, California, 59, *60*
Callan, Louise Smith, 31
Carrier, Betty Davis, 61, 63
Carter, W. A., 154
Carver, George Lee, 108
Cassidy, Butch, 146
Catholic Church, 4, 37, 115, 155
Center Ridge, Oregon, 119
Centerville School, California, *66*
Central School, Oregon, 129
chalkboards, 17, 18, 108, 136, 143. *See also* slates
Cheney Normal School, 153
Cherokee, 115
Cherokee Female Seminary, 115
Cherokee Male Seminary, 115
Cherry Creek School, California, 64
Cheyenne River Reservation, 132
Chicago, Rock Island and Pacific Railroad, 117
Chillicothe Ohio Teacher's College, 29

Chinese immigrants, 57, *57,* 100
Chiricahua Apaches, 41, *42*
chores
    as punishment, 17–18
    of students, 10, 11–12
    teachers and school maintenance, 15, 19
Christmas, 23, 62, 63, *112,* 134, 160
Christopher, Jeri, 30–31
Church of Jesus Christ of Latter-day Saints (Mormons), 41, 44, 74, 100, 144–47, 148
Cinnabar Basin School, Montana, 89
ciphering (arithmetic), 5, 15, 17, 83, 88, 116
citizenship, 132–34
clapboard construction, 8, 71, 78, 82, 93
Clarke, Abigail, 119
Clegg, Luther Bryan, 31
Clifton [Clifden] School, Texas, 138–41, *139, 140*
coal stoves, 8, 19, 72, 80, 131
Coeur d'Alene Reservation, 76
Coleman, John, 138
Collier, John, 44
Collins, Frances, 67
Colman Community Memorial Museum, *66*
Colorado
    history of, 69
    schoolhouses in, *9,* 69–74 *, 71, 73*
Colored School of Portland, Oregon, 129
Columbia Southern Railway, 124
common schools
    funding methods for, 5, 19
    public education history, 4, 118–19, 131, 134–35, 143–44, 154
    term definition, 5
community involvement, 22, 23
Congregational Church, 131, 143
Conroy, Everett, 27
Cooksey, Naomi, 58
corner standing, as punishment, 118
Cottonwood School, Texas, *141,* 141–42, *142*
Cowan, Mary, 12
cowboy students, 142
Cowley, Laura, 14–15
cow patties, 93

INDEX

Cox, Bill, 125
coyotes, 65
Crabtree, Lena, 67
Craig, Lee, 17–18
Crain, May, 127
Cramer, Emma, *17*
Crane, Oregon, 128
Creed, Walter, 27
crib books, 5, 6
Criterion School, Oregon, *126,* 126–27
Cross Hollows Stage Station, 124
Crow Valley School, Washington, 150
cultural assimilation policies
    of immigrants, 132–34
    of Native Americans, 37, 43, 44, 114
curriculum. *See also* learning models
    local governance of, 2
    standardization of, 4, 5, 7, 117
    subjects included in, 5, 15, 17, 31, 83, 88, 116
Curtis, Mrs. Frank E., 86
Custer, Clinton, *33*

Dakota Territory. *See* North Dakota; South Dakota
dances and dance halls, 126, 139, 146
Davis, Pearson, 80
day schools, 37, 114, 132, 154
Dayton, Nevada, *101,* 101–2, *102*
Deadrich, Katie, 135
deaf schools, 4, 106
DeCarlow, Charles, 125
DeCarlow, Lulu, 125–26
DeCartret, Miss, 30
Dennis, Lola, 143
Denny School, Oregon, *123*
Denton, Peggy Germolis, 12
deportment
    defined, 5, 17
    discipline methods, 17–18, *18,* 29, 118, 146, 147
Deseret School District, Utah, 147
desks, 1, *1, 68,* 135, 143, 146, 149
DeWitt, Lucy, 70
Diamond Hill School, Oregon, 123
Dickey, Mary E., 25
discipline, 17–18, *18,* 29, 118, 146, 147

District No. 1, Kansas, 82
Dixie School, The, California, 55, *56*
Doane College, 14
Dodge, Mary Abigail, 28–29
Doggett, Elisabeth Langdon, 21
Dolan, Marie, 120
Doniphan, Alexander, 108
Douglas Flat School, California, 50
Douglas Terrace School, North Dakota, 111
Drake, Martin, 125
Drake School, Oregon, 125
dress codes, *1, 2,* 31, 58
Drew School and Museum, Oregon, 128
dugout construction, 93
dunce hats, 17
Durham, Paradine, 141, *142*
Dutton, Joe, 88

Easley, Cheryl, 37, 39
Eastern Washington University, 153
East Fork School, California, 58
Eastman, Charles (Ohiyesa), 114
Eastman, Elaine Goodale, 114, *114*
Edsall, Fred, 125
Education (Brady), 95
Eisenhuth, Laura, 98
Eldean, Fred, 41
electricity, 49, 130
Elgin School, Nevada, 104
Ellensburg, Oregon, 123
Elmendorf, Armin, 136
Emet, Oklahoma, 116
Empty Schoolhouse, The (Clegg), 31
English Academy, Philadelphia, 4
Episcopal Church, 39–40, 154, *155*
Eskimos, 36
Esperanza School, Texas, 135
Euchle, Mrs., 138
Exodusters (Painter, N. I.), 82

fairs, as field trips, 25
Fargo, North Dakota, 111
Fiddletown School, 12
Fiddletown Schoolhouse Memories (Zorbas), 18, 30

INDEX

field trips, 25
Fine, Nancy, 128
Fiock, Charles H., 64, 65
Fiock, Mary, 65
fireplaces, 53
fires
    at Christmas programs, 23
    communities destroyed by, 49, 62, 74, 102
    orphanages destroyed by, 115
    safety prevention, 71, 150
    schoolhouses destroyed by, 62, 71, 86, 119, 121,
        122, 138, 147, 150
    transportation dangers due to, 78
floods, 52, 59, 68, 148
floors
    cleaning, as punishment, 17–18
    earthen, 42, 53, 78, 93
    platform standing, as punishment, 118
Ford, Henry, 2
Foreman, Picola, 31
Forks of Salmon School, California, 21, *22*
Fort Lupton Historic Park, 70
Fort Missoula, 86
Fort Owen, 86
Franklin, Benjamin, 4
Frazier, Maude, 21
Freeman, Daniel, 94
Freeman, Minnie, 95
Freeman, Thomas, 94
Freeman School, Nebraska, 94
Free Public School Act, 143
free schools, 115. *See also* common schools
French, Eugene, 62
Fruita School, Utah, 149
funding
    bonds, 52–53, 125, 135
    subscriptions, 5, 53, 111, 116, 127, 154
    taxes, 19, 135
furnishings
    benches, *1*, 121, 122
    blackboards, 17, 108, 118, 136, 143
    coal stoves, 8, 19, 72, 80, 131
    desks, 1, *1, 68,* 135, 143, 146, 149
    globes, 53, 146

lamps, kerosene, 80, 135
oil heaters, 63
Victrolas, 139
wood stoves, 1–2, 8, 31, 49, 127, 131, 135

Galena Creek Schoolhouse, Nevada, 103
Gallagher, F. M., 108
Gallaher, James Jackson, 122
Gallaher, William, 122
games, 88, 133, 152
geography, 31, 116
Georgetown School, Oklahoma, 2
German immigrants, 12, 36, 52, 74, 93, 132
German Lutheran School, Kansas, 78
Geronimo, 41, *42*
ghost towns, 40, 100, 119, 147
Gibson, Sandy, 88
Gioia, Lisa, 56
girls, 4, 11, 37, 58, 109
Glavich, Delbert, 30
Glendale, Nevada, 103
globes, 53, 146
Golconda School, Nevada, 102
gold
    in Alaska, 38
    in California, 24, 32, 44, *45*
    in Montana, 84
    in Nebraska, 92
    in Nevada, 101
    in Oregon, 44, 123
    in Wyoming, 156
Gold Beach, Oregon, 123
Goldenrod School, Iowa, 11
Golden Rule School, Kansas, 79, *79*
Gold Hill School, Colorado, 73–74
Goldrick, O. J., 72
Good, Joseph, 100
Goodsprings Mining District, The, 100
Goodsprings School, Nevada, 100
Goodsprings Township, Nevada, 100
Goodwill, Adelaide, 93
Gore, Walter, 127
grades, 116
Grafton, Utah, 147–48

INDEX

Grand Junction School, Colorado, *9*
Granlee Gulch School, Colorado, 70, *71*
Grant Creek School, Montana, 86
Great Depression, 120, 131, 133
Grupé, Laurie, 126
Guhin, Michael M., 132
Guinn, J. M., 52–53
Gulliford, Andrew, 85, 104
guns, 121, 142

Hadl, Leonard, 80
Hall, Julia, 131
Hallock, Elsie Petsel, 21
Hamilton, P. R., 53
Harmony School, Nebraska, 97
Harney County, Oregon, 128
Harris, Benjamin, 7
Harris, California, 58
Harrison School, Oregon, 129
Hart, William, slates of, *17*
Harte, Bret, 55, *55*
Harvard College, 4
Havasupai, 43
Hawaiian immigrants, 64, *64*
Hawthorne School, North Dakota, 111
Hayden, Robin, 59, *60*
Hayden, Shawn, 59, *60*
heating
    coal, 8, 19, 72, 80, 131
    cow patties, 93
    oil, 63
    wood, 1–2, 8, 31, 49, 72, 135, 136
Helotes School, Texas, 136, *137, 138*
Henderson, Floyd, 109
High, Geneive, 67
Hillerman, Tony, 2
Hollenberg, G. H., 97
Holtman, Annie, 152
Homecoming, 82
Homestead Act, 32–34, 77, 78, 84, *85,* 108
Honolulu School, California, 64, *64*
Hooperville School, California, *3*
Hopi, 43
Hoppe, Hugo, 89

hornbooks, 5, 6
horses
    anecdotes about, 56
    lunchtime picnics, 138
    rules on, 11
    student transportation, 11, 25, 56, 58, 62, 71, 152
    teacher-student recreation, 160
    teacher transportation, 25, 127
Howard, Lucy, 98
Howard School, Oregon, 119
Hualapai Indians, 43, 44
Huey, Major, 30
Huey, Queen, 67
Huffman, Lester, 56
Humbug School, California, 27, *27*
humiliation, as discipline method, 17, 149
Humphrey Heritage Village, 117
Hunsley, Melissa, *112*
hunting, 30
Hurlbut, Grace, 97, *97*
Huston, Susie, 88
Hutterites, 132

Idaho
    class photos of students, *76, 77*
    history of, 74
    immigrant populations, 74, 82
    schoolhouses in, 74–77, *76, 77*
Igo Schoolhouse, California, 49, *49*
immigrants
    in Alaska, 34, 35–36, *36*
    in California, 52, 57, *57,* 64
    in Colorado, 12, 14
    in Idaho, 74, 82
    in Nebraska, 93
    in Nevada, 101
    South Dakota education policies, 132–34
    as westward movement influence, 34
    World War I and perception of, 132
Independence School, Colorado, 69–70
Indian Intertribal Council, 115
Indian Park School, Colorado, 70
Indian Territory, Oklahoma, 115–16
Indigenous Healing, 39

Indio schoolhouse, California, 52
inkwells, 146
integration, 128
intermarriages, *47,* 47–48, 114
International Order of Odd Fellows (IOOF), 100
Irish immigrants, 34
Italian immigrants, 132
It's Me, May I Come In? (Fiock), 64

Jackson, Loretta, 117
Jackson, Lucy, 53
Jackson, Sheldon, 38
Jackson County School District #94, Oregon, 125–26
Jarre Canon School, Colorado, 70
Jefferson, Thomas, 4
Jenner, GloryAnn (Colt), 59, *60*
Jenny Creek Slide, 125
Jensen, Mary, 29
Johannsen, Pete, 120
Johnson, Lyndon Baines, 135–36
Johnson, Thomas, 79
Jones, Steven F., 78
Junction School, California, 21
Junction School, Texas, 135–36

Kanakas, 64
Kansas
    African American communities in, *81,* 81–82
    class photos of students, *79, 80*
    female county superintendents in, 98
    history of, 78
    immigrant population, 34
    Native American boarding schools in, 79
    school construction materials, 78
    schoolhouses in, 78–84, *84*
    Sunday school classes, *80*
    teachers in, 78, 83, *83*
Kansas-Nebraska Act, 78
Kao Ming School, California, 57
Kearny, Stephen W., 108
Keller Heritage Center, 150–51
Kennedy, Lois, 12–13, *14*
Kennett Schoolhouse, California, *59*

Kenyon School, California, 21, 25
Kings Valley School, Oregon, 120
Kipp family, 86
Kirwin, William, 156–57
Kirwin, Wyoming, 156
Kissick, Minnie, *80*
Kleaver, Bill, 17
Kuelp, Fred William, 52

La Belle, Jim, 39
Labouchere Bay School, Alaska, 40
ladders, 71, *94*
La Grange School, California, 55, *55*
Laguna Elementary, California, 58
Lagunita Schoolhouse, California, *66*
Lame Johnny School, South Dakota, 131
lamps, kerosene, 80, 135
Lanesfield School, Kansas, 80
Lansford, Lynn Milburn, 116
Larson, Lars and Belle, 106
Latin Grammar School, Massachusetts, 4
learning models
    field trips and experiential, 25
    fluidity of, 90–91
    for immigrant education, 133
    innovative, 88
    oral, 5, 15
    repetition and recitation, 6, 15, 121
Leary, Josephine Codoni, 55
Lebanon School, Colorado, 71–72, *73*
Leffingwell, George, 11
Lehi School, Arizona, 42–43
Leitz, Glenn, 152
Lewis and Clark Expedition, 74
libraries, 130
lightning, 80
limestone construction, 78, 136
Lincoln, Abraham, 2, 32–33
Lincoln School, North Dakota, 111
Litster, Phoebe C., 146–47
Little House on the Prairie (Wilder), 2
Lively, William, 143
lizards, 30
Lochiel, Arizona, 40

log construction, 8, 76, 111, 120, 121, 122, 128, 135, 145, 148, 149, 152
log house construction, as recess activity, 152
Logtown School District, Oregon, 125
Lone Pine School, Oregon, 120
Longfellow School, North Dakota, 111
Loretta Y. Jackson Historical Society, 117
Los Reyes schools, Texas, 136
Lost Creek, Oregon, 119
Lower Fox Creek School, Kansas, 78
Lower Shell School, Wyoming, *156, 157*
Lubenko, Mitch, 18
Lugg, Charles L., 131
lunches, 31, 72, 159
Lyndon B. Johnson National Historical Park, 136
Lyons, Ruth, 72

Mac and Muff (pre-primer series), 88
Madla, Frank, 136
Malmberg, Norm, 11
Mann, Horace, 4, 19
Mann Creek Schoolhouse, 74
Maplesden, Carol Pitts, 58
marriage, 2, *47,* 47–48, 114
Masons, 87, *87,* 89, 100
Massachusetts, 4
Massey, Cynthia Leal, 136
math, 5, 15, 17, 83, 88, 116
Maude Frazier: Nevadam (Frazier), 21
May School, Nebraska, *99*
McBride, Bud, 150
McClelland, Betty Trueau, 152
McCraig, Mary M., 56
McCreary, Betty, 135
McGuffey Reader, 7, *7*
McKenzie, Richard, 135
McKinley, William, 43
McKinley School, North Dakota, 111
Meamber, Fern, 61
Medford, Oregon, 127
Meeteetse, Wyoming, 155–56
Memoirs of South Dakota Retired Teachers, 131
Mennonite Heritage Museum, 83
Mennonites, 82–83, 119

Mercer, T. Lillie, 42
Methodist Church, 143
Mexican-American War, 32, 92, 108
Milburn: The Birth of a Pioneer Town and the Love Story that Began There (Lynn Milburn Lansford), 116
Milburn, W. J., 116
Milburn Son, Alma Jane, 116
Miller, Ellen Independence, 55
Miller, James, 55
Minersville School, California, 10
mining
  in Alaska, *35,* 40
  California, 24, 32, 44, *45*
  in California, 44, *45*
  in Idaho, 75
  in Nevada, 100, 101, *101*
  in Oregon, 44, 123
  in Wyoming, 156
missionary schools
  in Alaska, 37, 38, 39
  in California, 45
  in North Dakota, 109
  in South Dakota, 132
  in Utah, 143
  in Washington, 149
  in Wyoming, 154, 155, *155*
Mission Boarding School, Wyoming, *155*
Mission Dolores, 45
Mission Santa Clara, 45
Mission School, Alaska, 37
Missouri, 11, 78, 93, 108
Missouri Mounted Volunteers, 108
Mittelstadt, John, 107
Model School Score Card, 117
Moe, Eleanore Rowan, 134
Moffett Creek School, California, *17*
Molly Logan mine, 156
Mono School, California, 64
Montana
  education policies, 85
  history of, 84, *85*
  modern use of one-room schools in, 92, *159*
  oldest standing school, 86

school districts, first, 86
schoolhouses in, 85–91, *87, 90, 91, 159*
school names, 85
schools and student statistics, 85
student experiences, 11, 90–91
teaching experiences, 158–60
Yellowstone National Park, 89
Moody, O. H., 97, *98*
Moore, Kathy, 59, *60*
moral character, 6–7, 134, 153
Morales, Lorenzo, 136
Mora Schoolhouse, Idaho, 75
Morgan, Norma and Gilbert, 122
Mormons, 41, 44, 74, 100, 144–47, 148
Morris, Emma, 83, *83, 84*
Morris, Helen Hussman, 117–18
Moulton, Larry, 130
Mountain School, Colorado, 70
Mount Turnbull, Arizona, 41
Muelrath, Cicely, 12
Munger, Charles, 82
Munn, Vella, *23,* 23–24
Murdock Academy, Utah, 147

Nash, M. A., 117
Native Americans. *See also* boarding schools
    day schools for, 37, 114, 132, 154
    education policies on, 38, 109, 114, 131
    government policies toward, 37, 44, 115, 131
    healing programs for, 39–40
    Idaho statistics, 74
    interracial marriages, *47,* 47–48
    missionary schools for, 37, 38, 39, 109, 132, 149,
        154, 155, *155*
    settler conflicts with, 123
    as teachers, 129, 149
    traditional territories and sacred mountains of,
        104, *105*
    Yellowstone National Park history and, 89
Navajo, 43, 104, *105,* 107, *107,* 108
Nebraska
    class photos of students, *99*
    first school in, 93
    history of, *92,* 92–93

modern use of one-room schools in, 2, 99
school construction style and materials, 93
schoolhouses in, 93–94, *94, 99,* 100
superintendents in, 98
teacherages, 93
teacher experiences, *14,* 14–15
teacher gender statistics, *99*
teaching certificates, 97, *97, 98*
winter conditions, 95
Nebraska marble, 78
Nelson, Mercy, 111
Nevada
    history of, 100–102, *101*
    immigrant populations, 101
    modern use of one-room schoolhouses in, 100
    schoolhouses in, 100–104
    school relocations, 103, 104
    teacherages, 104
    teaching experiences in, 21
New England Primer (Harris), 7
New Hope School, Texas, 143
New Mexico
    battleground schools, 108
    deaf schools, 106
    history of, 104, *105, 106*
    native populations and boarding schools in, 104,
        107, *107,* 108
    outdoor museums with schools, 105
New Mexico School for the Deaf (NMSD), 106
Newton, Lester E., 30, 158
Nicodemus, Kansas, *81,* 81–82
Niza, Marcos de, 40
normal schools
    enrollment criteria, 153
    history of, 4
    in North Dakota, 109
    in Ohio, 29
    in Oklahoma, 115
    program descriptions, 5, 14, 29
    terminology origins, 153
    in Washington, 153, *153*
North Dakota
    Christmas celebrations, *112*
    first schools in, 109, 110

history of, 108–9, *110*
immigrant population, 34, 132
Native American day schools, 114
orphanage/free schools, 115
school barns, *113*
schoolhouses in, 89–91, *90,* 109, 110–12, *113*
teacher certification and demographics, 109
Northeastern State Normal School (*now*
    Northeastern State University), 115
Northern Pacific Railroad, 89, 111, 153
North School, Oregon, 129

Oak Grove School, Oregon, 121
Oakland School, Oregon, 130
Oates, Joyce Carol, 2
O'Connor, Hugh and Denis, 120
Ohio, 29, 122
Ohiyesa (Charles Eastman), 114
oil heaters, 63
Ojo Sarco one-room school, New Mexico, 108
Oklahoma
    African-American schools in, 117
    class photos of students, *118*
    education policies, 117
    history of, 115–16
    native populations in, 115
    normal schools in, 115
    schoolhouses in, 2, 116, 117, *118*
    schools relocated, 117
    school statistics, 117
    student experiences, 116
    student statistics, 117
    teaching experiences in, 117–18
Old Brazito Schoolhouse, The, New Mexico, 108
Old Deluder Satan Act, 4
Old Santa Fe Trail, The (Remington), *106*
Old School, South Dakota, *133*
Old Schoolhouse, The, Nevada, 103
Old Star School, Montana, 85–86
Olson, Charles, 120–21
Olympia, Washington, 149
One-Room Country School: South Dakota Stories, 133,
    134
oral teaching, 5, 15

Orcas Island Historical Museum, 150
Oregon
    African-American schools in, 128–29, *129*
    class photos of students, *123*
    education costs, 129
    education policies, 118–19
    ghost towns of, 119
    history of, 44, 123, 124, 127, 130
    modern use of one-room schools in, 120, 126
    native conflicts in, 123
    schoolhouses in, 119–20, 121–22, 124–30, *126*
    student experiences, 12, 120–21, 124, 128–30
    teaching experiences, 30–31, 119
Organic Act, 38, 39
Orion school, Oklahoma, 118
orphanages, 39, 115
Otero, Sabino, 42
Ott, Margaret, 29
Our Common Schools (Dodge), 28–29
Outhouse, John W., 119
outhouses
    cleaning, as punishment, 18
    double-seaters, 71
    pranks using, 30
    at schools, 49, 62, 63, 80, 88, *94,* 130, 136
    winter temperatures and, 72
overalls, 58
Oysterville School, Washington, *151*

pack train transportation, 21, 22
Painter, Erik, 104, 107
Painter, Nell Irvin, 82
Papag Indians, 43
parents, 18, 23, 159
Peers, Michael, 39–40
Pehl, John, 135
Pehrson, Nolan, 25
Pembina, North Dakota, 109
penmanship, 15
Pennsylvania, 4
Pepperwood School, California, *68*
Percival, D. F., 153
Permanent School Fund, 135
Peterson, Augustus, 143

Phelps, Lanora, 61

Phoenix Indian School, Arizona, 43, *44*

picnics, 138

Pima Indians, 43

Pinehurst School: 100 Years of Growing up on the Greensprings (Slater), 125

Pine Ridge Reservation, 109, 131–32

Pinhurst School, Oregon, 125–26

Pinkham, Alvira, 111

Pinkham, Francis, 111

Pioneer School, Alaska, 36–37

Pioneer Stories of Cass County, Nebraska (Cass County Historical Society), 92

Pioneer Village (Zilker Botanical Garden), 135

Pitts, Mary, 58

platform standing, as punishment, 118

playgrounds, *13, 22, 64,* 91, 117

playrooms, 62, 63

Pleasant Valley School, Oklahoma, 117

Pleasant Valley School, Washington, 150

plumbing, indoor, 72, 130, 150

Polk, James, 108

Ponce de Leon, Antonio, 108

Prairie View School, Washington, 152

pranks, 21, 27, 30

Presbyterian Church, 37, 143

Presbyterian Mission School, Alaksa, 37

Presentation Sisters, 115

primers (readers), 5, 7, *7,* 88

principals, 31, 52, 127, 147

public education

    funding methods for, 5, 19

    history of, 4, 118–19, 131, 134–35, 143–44, 154

    term definition, 5

punishment, 17–18, *18,* 29, 118, 146, 147

Pursel, Ina Stocker, 125

Pursel, Nelson, 127

Rae, Mae, 143

railroads

    community development dependent on, 82, 89

    community development due to, 74, 80, 89, 109, 116, 117, 124, 127, 144, 150

property provided by, 111

school construction by, 117

train anecdotes, 116

Ralston, Leslie, 25

Rancho de las Golondrinas, El, 105

Ranney, Grace Ann, 53

Rapp, Sally, 129

rats, 78, 93, 159

rattlesnakes, 31, 53

readers (primers), 5, 7, *7,* 88

reading

    books for, 5, 7, *7,* 88

    classroom libraries for, 130

    as curriculum requirement, 15, 116

Reagan, Ronald, 44

recesses

    activities during, 59, 152

    horse management requirements during, 72

    inclement weather options, 62, 63

    playgrounds, *13, 22, 54,* 91, 117

    winter recreation during, 91

recitation (learning model), 5, 6, 15, 121

Red-Brick School House, Nebraska, 93–94

Red Pony, The (Steinbeck), 66

Red Prairie School, Texas, 143

Remington, Frederic: *The Old Santa Fe Trail, 106*

Reminiscences of the Past of Siskiyou County (French), 62

repetition (learning model), 6, 15, 121

restrooms, 72, 130. *See also* outhouses

Riggs, Kate and James, 136

Riversdale School, Oregon, 129–30

Riverside School, California, 17

Robert, Emily, 30

Roberts, John, 155

Roce, Lois May, 95

rock construction, 139, *140*

Rock Hill School, Oregon, 121–22

Rock Island and Pacific Railroad, 117

Rocky Mountain School, California, 30

Rocky Ridge School, North Dakota, 112, *112*

Rogers, Ruth, 58

Rogue River Indians, 123

role modeling, 19

Roman Catholic Mission of the Holy Cross, Alaska, 37

Roosevelt School, California, 52

Roosevelt School, North Dakota, 111

Rose Hill School, Oklahoma, 117

Ross School, California, 64

Rowan School, South Dakota, 134

Royce, Florence, 87

Ruch District, Oregon, 125

rulers, as disciplinary tools, 118, 146, 147

rules and regulations
    discipline for breaking, 17–18, *18*, 29, 118, 146, 147
    horse racing, 11
    for teachers, 19, *20*, 21

Russian immigrants, 82

Sandell, Cindy (Irene), 141–42

Sand Springs School, Montana, 88, 158–60, *159*

San Francisco, California, 44–45

Santa Fe Railroad, 116

Santa Fe Trail, 105, *106*, 108

Sato, Carolyn, 41

Scandinavian immigrants, 36

Scherneckau, August, 124

Schneider, Richard, 150

"Schoolchildren's Blizzard, The," 95, *96*

School District #53, Nebraska, 97

schoolhouses, overview
    atmosphere of, 12, 91
    building materials used for, 8, 78, 93
    current statistics, 2
    daily schedule, 11
    early twentieth-century statistics, 2
    interior views of, *1*
    maintenance of, 15, 19
    school year and terms of, 8

schoolmarms
    as career choice, 21
    experiences of, 14–15, 30–31
    gender and preference for, 19
    gender comparison statistics, 21
    marital status requirements, 2

poems about, 28–29, 83

as principals, 31

rules for, 19, *20,* 21

salaries of, 22, 31, 78, 80, 119, 149

as superintendents, 98

schoolmasters, 21, 82, 119, 149

Schott, August D., 138, 139

Schott, Betty Lou, 139

Schott, Hank, and family, 139

Schott, Howard W., 139, 141

Schott, Leora, *140*

Schott, Peggy, 139

Scott, Bev, 97–98

Scott, Bill, 83

Scott, Eva Ellen Russell, 98

Searle, Annie Rosetta, 146

seating, 15, 135, 149

Secrest, Sarah, 11

Semple, Robert, 48–49

sentence writing, as punishment, 29

Shake, Oregon, 125

Shaniko, Oregon, 124–25

Sharping, Evelyn Myers, 133

Shasta River School, California, *63,* 64, 65

Shaw Island School, Washington, 150

Shawnee Indian Mission School, Kansas, 78, 79

Sherman Station Visitor's Center, 103

Shiprock, 104, *105*

Shlaudeman, Dawn, 158

shoelessness, *1,* 2, 31

Short, Howard, 112, *113*

Short, Kayann, 112

Short, Russell, 112, *112, 113*

Shoshone, 89, 155, *155*

Shoshone Episcopal Mission, *155*

Shoshone River Mining Company, 156

Siletz Indians, 123

Sioux Indians, 114

Siskiyou County Museum, 56

Sisters of Charity, 155

Sisters of the Order of Saint Ursula, 4

Sitka Industrial Training School, 37

skunks, 30, 31

Slater, Aleatha, 124

INDEX

slates, 1, 5, 15, *16,* 17
slavery, 32, 122
slaves, free, 114
Smith, Kermit, 112, *113*
Smith, Minnie, *22*
Smith, Ralph and Gil, 21
Smith, William, 70
Smuggler mine, 156
snakes, 78, 93
Soap Creek School, Oregon, 120–21
sod construction ("soddies"), 8, *9,* 78, 93, 109
South Carolina, 4
South Dakota
    blizzards of, *96,* 134
    Christmas celebrations, 134
    class photos of students, *133*
    education policies, 114, 131, 132–34
    history of, 131
    immigrant Americanization education, 132–34
    Native American schools, 131–32
    schoolhouses in, *133,* 134
    school programs, 134
    school statistics, 131
    superintendents, 131
    teacherage statistics, 150
    teacher experiences, 15, 131
Spalding, H. H., 149
Spalding, Hannah C., 74
spanking, 17, 18, 118
spelling, 116
Spokane, Washington, 149, 150
Spokan Garry, 149
sports, 12
Spring Schoolhouse, California, 56
Squaw Gap School, Montana, 89–91, *90*
St. John's Orphanage and Free School, North
    Dakota, 115
standardization, 4, 5, 7, 117
Starritt, Minerva, 22–23
Steele Indian School Park, 44
Steinbeck, John, 66
Stermitz, Joseph, Sr., 89
Stevens County Historical Society Museum, 151
Stocker, Ina, 127

stone construction, 103, 150
Stone Lagoon School, California, *69*
stoves
    coal, 8, 19, 72, 80, 131
    wood, 1–2, 8, 31, 49, 127, 131, 135, 136
straw-bale construction, 93
Strawberry Schoolhouse, Arizona, 40–41
Stronk, Belle, 127
students
    classroom views with, *1, 68*
    class sizes, 22, 23, 67, 88, 90, 119, 136, 158
    cowboys as, 142
    deportment and discipline, 17–18, *18,* 29, 118,
      146, 147
    with disabilities, 4, 106
    dress codes, 58
    education experiences of, 12, 61–63, 150–52
    experiences of, 11, 12, 61–63, 90–91, 116,
      120–21, 124, 128–30, 150–52
    gender and education expectations, 11
    pranks, 21, 27, 30
    responsibilities of, 10, 11–12
    turnover, 30
subscriptions, 5, 53, 111, 116, 127, 154
summer schools, 21–22
summer terms, 8, 111
summer weather, 8, 78
Sumner, Charles, 34
Sunday school, 50, *80,* 126, 156
superintendents, 70, 97, 98, 122
supplies, 2, 15, 108, 129
Sutter Grammar Creek School, California, 52
Sweet Briar School, North Dakota, 111

Tablerock Schoolhouse, California, *61,* 63
Tahlequah, Oklahoma, 115
Talent Elementary School, Oregon, 124
Taylor, Diane Biggar, 150–51, 152
teacherages
    definition, 5
    descriptions, 21, 88, 93, 104, 105, 159
    origins of, 150
    in South Dakota, statistics, 150
teacher contracts, *20*

teacher residences. *See also* teacherages
  cabins, 21
  with families, 21, 29, 31, 150
  hotels, 21
  in school board president's house, 14
  in unfinished attics, 131
teachers. *See also* normal schools; schoolmarms;
    schoolmasters; teacher residences
  continuing education of, 26–27
  early legislation and community requirements
    of, 4
  education of, 4
  gender statistics, 21
  influence of, 19, 72
  job descriptions and duties of, 15, 19, 29, 78
  rotation of, 2
  rules for, 2, 19, *20*, 21
  salaries of, 22, 31, 78, 80, 82, 119, 149
  training, 4
teachers institutes, 26–27
teaching certificates, 97, *97, 98*
teaching schools. *See* normal schools
Tewksbury, Charles, 157
Texas
  class photos of students, *137, 139, 140, 142*
  education policies, 134–35
  schoolhouses in, 135–43, *137, 138, 141*
  teacher experiences, 31, 142
  water pumps, *140*
  wildlife encounters, 31
textbooks, 2, 5, 7, *7*, 117, 132
Thomas, Heidi, 88, 159
Thomas County School, Kansas, 78
Three Rs of education, 15
Tillamook Indians, 123
Tinneh Indians, 36
Tison, Henry, Jr., 128
Tison, Henry Clay, 128
Tlingit, 36, 37, 40
Tohono O'odham Indians, 43
toilet tipping pranks, 30
Tolowa Indians, 123
Torrey Log Church–Schoolhouse, Utah, 148
Townsley, Mabel, 15

trains, 116. *See also* railroads
transportation of students. *See also* walking to school
  buses, 11, 59, 72
  field trips and open touring cars, 25, *26*
  by horseback, 11, 25, 56, 58, 62, 71, 152
  as teacher's responsibility, 29, 127
transportation of teachers
  by horseback, 25, 127
  by pack train, 21, 22
  to teacher institutes, *26, 26*–27
  winter challenges, 21
Truxton Canyon Training School, Arizona, 43, *43,
    44*
Tubac School, Arizona, 42
Tuggle, Kenneth, 80
Tumlum mine, 156
Turkey Creek School, Oklahoma, 117
Twight-Alexander, Susanne, *50*

Underground Railroad, 122
Union School, Colorado, 72
United Brethren Church, 122
United States Industrial Indian School, Arizona,
    43, *44*
University of Pennsylvania, 4
Ustick, Harlan Page, 75
Ustick School, Idaho, 75
Utah
  class photos of students, *144*
  education policies, 143
  history of, 143–49, *144, 145, 147*
  missionary schools, 143
  native populations, 104
  schoolhouses in, 147–49
  secondary schools, 144
  teachers of, *144*, 144–47, *145, 147*

Valley City Normal School, 109
Verden Separate School, Oklahoma, 117
vernacular construction, 5, 93
Vernal School, Utah, 145
Vernon School, California, 53
Victrolas, 139
Villa, Pancho, 40

INDEX

Virginia, 4
Virginia City, Montana, 86
vocabulary, 88
"Voices of our Elders" project, 37

Walapai (Hualapai) Indians, 44
walking to school
    distances, 11, 14, 31, 65, 71, 91, 116, 131, 136,
      152
    train incidents, 116
    wildlife encounters, 65, 121
    winter conditions, 65, 95, *96*
Walla Walla, Washington, 149
Waneta School, Texas, 143
Washington
    first schools, 149–50
    Native American schools, 149
    normal schools in, 153, *153*
    schoolhouses in, 150–52, *151*
    school statistics, 150
    student experiences, 150–52
    student statistics, 150
    teacherages, first built, 150
    teachers in, 149
Washington Bar School, California, *23*, 23–24
Washington School, North Dakota, 111
Washoe City, Nevada, 100
water supply
    buckets, 49
    none, 159
    pumps, 140
    urns, 2
    wells, 63, 72, 75, 80, 136
weather, 8, 78. *See also* winter
Weatherford, James Knox Polk, 122
Weaverville Courthouse, *68*
Weber, Linda Jones, 129–30
Weiser School District, Idaho, 74
Wendt, Fred, 139
Western Pacific Railroad, 109
West Vermillion School, South Dakota, 131
westward movement, 19, 32–34, 44, 47–48, 115, 125
Wheeler, Jane and J. J., 42
Wheeling, Joe, 89–90

Whitman, Marcus, 149
Wilder, Laura Ingalls, 2
Williamson, William A., 127
Willis, Bob and Flora, 126
Willow Creek School, California, *57*
Wilson, Sophia, 127
window washing, as punishment, 18
Wind River Reservation, 154, 155
winter
    blizzard conditions, 95, *96*, 134, 157
    building construction and temperature control,
      78
    chores during, 12
    heating challenges, 2, 8, 10, 24
    outhouses during, 72
    recess recreation during, 91
    transportation difficulties, 10, 21
    walking to school in, 65, 95, *96*
Winton Elementary, Washington, 150
wolves, 121
women. *See also* schoolmarms
    homestead claims by, 33–34, 77
    husband-seeking, 48, *48*
    interracial marriages, *47*, 47–48
wood-frame construction, *76*, 93, 102, 110, 120,
    122, 124, 130, 136, 150
wood stoves, 1–2, 8, 31, 49, 127, 131, 135, 136
wood supplies, 10, 15, 18, 127
Woodward, Don Carlos, 145
Woodward, Maude, *147*
Woodward, Robert Lewis, *144*, 144–47, *145*, *147*
Woodward, Rosetta, *147*
Wooster, Quincy A., 143
Wooster Common School No. 38, 143
World War I, 2, 125, 132
WPA (Works Progress Administration), 111, 157
Wrangell Institute Boarding School, 39
Wright, C. C., 55
Wyandotte School, California, *54*
Wyoming
    education policies, 154, 157
    history of, 154–57
    immigrant population, 34
    mining history, 156

modern use of one-room schools in, 2
Native American schools in, 154, 155, *155*
native populations in, 154, 155
schoolhouses in, *154,* 154–55, *155, 156,* 157, *157*
school statistics, 157
student statistics, 157
superintendents in, 98
teachers in, statistics, 157

Yank, Irene, 21
yardsticks, as disciplinary tools, 17, 118
Yavapai, 43

YCL (Young Citizens League), 132–34
Yellow Pine Mining District, The, 100
Yellowstone National Park, 89
Yerba Buena, California, 44–45
Yoder School, Oregon, 119
Young, Jolyn, 12
Young Citizens League (YCL), 132–34
Young Ladies Academy, Philadelphia, 4

Zenger, Eliza Ann, 77
Zilker Botanical Garden, 135
Zoller, Henry, 86
Zorbas, Elaine, 18

About the Author

Gail L. Jenner is the author of six nonfiction histories and two historical novels. In addition, *One Room: Schools and Schoolteachers of the Pioneer West* is the fourth book she has authored for TwoDot/Globe Pequot.

Gail writes for NPR/Jefferson Public Radio's historical series as well as for a regional publication. She has appeared on History Channel's *How the States Got Their Shapes*, on Fox's *Legends and Lies: Black Bart*, and on *Mysteries at the Museum*, on NPR's *West Coast Live*, and she contributed to Huell Howser's public television special, *California Gold: The State of Jefferson*. In addition, she has contributed to a number of anthologies and magazines.

Her work has won or placed in a number of award competitions, including the 2017 IPPY Bronze Award, the 2002 WILLA Literary Award, the William Faulkner Literary Short Story Contest, two Writer's Digest Competitions, and others.

Gail is the wife of a fourth-generation cattle rancher. They live on the original Jenner family homestead where history is a part of everyday life. She is also a former secondary history and English teacher. A gardener and cook, she enjoys cooking for ranch hands, family, and friends, and especially enjoys working and spending time on the ranch.

She is a member of Western Writers of America, Women Writing the West, and several other organizations.